OGC Portfolio Product

Agile Project and Service Management: delivering IT services using ITIL®, PRINCE2™ and DSDM® Atern®

London: TSO

Published by TSO (The Stationery Office) and available from:

Online
www.tsoshop.co.uk

Mail, Telephone, Fax & E-mail
TSO
PO Box 29, Norwich, NR3 1GN
Telephone orders/General enquiries: 0870 600 5522
Fax orders: 0870 600 5533
E-mail: customer.services@tso.co.uk
Textphone: 0870 240 3701

TSO@Blackwell and other Accredited Agents

Customers can also order publications from:
TSO Ireland
16 Arthur Street, Belfast BT1 4GD
Tel: 028 9023 8451 Fax: 028 9023 5401

A CIP catalogue record for this book is available from the British Library

A Library of Congress CIP catalogue record has been applied for

First published 2010

ISBN 9780113310975

Printed in the United Kingdom by The Stationery Office, London
P002363455   c6   07/10   4072

Contents

List of figures

List of tables

Acknowledgements

ABOUT THE AUTHOR

Dorothy Tudor is a director of TCC Ltd, a leading training and consultancy company operating worldwide with expertise in PRINCE2™, DSDM® Atern® and ITIL®. She has worked on agile projects at large financial institutions, technology companies and public-sector organizations, among others. She is a DSDM Atern practitioner, PRINCE2 project manager and ITIL service manager. A thought leader, she is active in the project community and has authored many articles and publications. For further details visit www.tcc-net.com.

REVIEWERS

The author and The Stationery Office (TSO) would like to thank the following for their helpful comments in reviewing drafts of this work.

Julia Godwin	Be Consulting Ltd Director
Hugh Ivory	Best Outcomes Director; DSDM Director
Tony Jenkins	Information Systems Examining Board (ISEB) Examiner
Steve Messenger	Napp Pharmaceutical Holdings Ltd; DSDM Consortium Chairman
Barbara Roberts	Independent Atern Consultant; DSDM Consortium Director
Steve Tremblay	Excelsa Technologies Consulting Inc.

The author would also like to thank Jerry Humphreys, Rob Shipley, Ian Tudor, Jonathan Tudor and Mark Tudor for reviewing the publication and making valuable comments and additions.

CASE STUDY ACKNOWLEDGEMENTS

The author would like to thank Allied Irish Banks, AQA, Hampshire County Council and the Met Office for sharing their experiences for Chapter 12 of this publication and, in particular, the following people for their time, assistance and insight into their organization's journey towards adoption of ITIL, PRINCE2 and DSDM Atern:

Allied Irish Banks

David Barron	IT Service Control Manager
Gina Lordan	Service Improvement Manager
Mairéad Reid	SDLC Support Team
Eddie Sweeney	General Manager, Enterprise Systems & Technology

AQA

Vidal Brownlee	Head of ISD

Hampshire County Council

Ian Barnett	Project Office and previously Project Manager of ITIL Implementation

Mike Russell	Head of Products and Services Team
Mike Stevens	Project Office and Service Planning Manager

The Met Office

Gary Auger	DSDM Atern
Nina Hartley	P3M Guardian of Profession
Malcolm Lee	Project management process
Anthea Nelson	Service management
Nigel Reed	Service development

Preface

WHY READ THIS PUBLICATION?

The need to manage and sustain IT services, whilst at the same time reacting quickly to ever-changing external environments is probably, for many, the real driver for reading this publication.

ITIL (v3), PRINCE2 (2009) and DSDM Atern (v2) are the leading best-practice approaches for delivering business change and managing IT services. They are widely used throughout the UK and beyond, and most companies are influenced by some or all of the approaches, either directly or via their customers or suppliers. Many organizations have already implemented one or two of these three approaches and are now looking at extending this further, with the addition of another of the three. Each approach has strengths from which an organization can benefit.

ITIL is the overarching framework for the effective management of IT services. However, it does not provide guidance on the management of the change projects that happen within its domain. PRINCE2 has great strength and control in project governance, but is perceived as a sequential, waterfall process, which is slow to react to change. DSDM Atern is an agile project management framework, which embraces change. It promotes incremental delivery, prioritization and iterative development, focused on providing early business value. It is uncompromising in its approach to the quality of deliverables, and experience shows that it is capable of working well in highly regulated environments. It has something to bring to both the project and service management cultures.

This publication will show the reader how to combine these three approaches effectively and get the best out of their structure and agility.

INTRODUCTION

Welcome to the world of effective IT service management and of on-time, on-budget delivery of projects, which really do meet the business need and deliver value early and frequently! This publication looks at how effective IT service management can be achieved using three best-practice frameworks:

- ITIL (v3) – a framework for managing the provision of IT services
- PRINCE2 (2009) – a structured project management approach suitable for all types of project
- DSDM Atern (v2) – an agile project delivery framework, suitable for all types of project.

Individually, ITIL, PRINCE2 and DSDM Atern are powerful approaches built by practitioners for practitioners. Together they are even more potent – the whole is greater than the sum of its parts.

Today's organizations have to make huge investments in IT systems to support their business and remain competitive in a world of rapid change. They need to be able to sustain these systems effectively and be responsive to the frequent need for change. An ad hoc approach to providing consistent and reliable services and managing change projects is just not an option. It is vital for an organization to focus sharply on business value, good return on investment, speed to market, and delivery of solutions in response to change. Understanding and employing the best-practice approaches of ITIL and PRINCE2 together can provide the foundations for a well-run IT infrastructure and well-controlled projects. The addition of DSDM Atern, an agile project management framework, encourages an incremental approach to change, resulting in risk reduction and early, frequent delivery of business value. By applying ITIL guidance together with the PRINCE2 and DSDM Atern approaches, an environment can be established where IT service provision is reliable, cost-effective and responsive to change, and projects are delivered, under control, and consistently producing the right results on time and on budget.

This publication offers practical guidance on how to deliver an IT service by employing ITIL, PRINCE2 and DSDM Atern together. It discusses all three approaches separately, providing an overview of each. It considers the benefits of each approach and also describes any issues that may arise. It addresses how they fit together, where they overlap and where the needs for each exist, in a way that gives guidance on how to implement one, two or all three of the approaches.

STRUCTURE

The publication has been structured to appeal to those considering one, two or all three of the approaches. Some chapters concentrate on the practical use of the approaches and some are summaries of the pure approaches (theory). Each theory chapter is an easy reference point and gives a brief overview of the key elements of the approach. The reader knowledgeable in a particular approach may wish to skip the theory chapter for that approach, or use it as a quick refresher. Interspersed with the theory chapters, we follow the journey of a fictitious company, 'Octagrid', as a vehicle for consolidating practical experiences drawn from several real companies. To create this hybrid company, the author has researched extensively within all sectors and the story of Octagrid is told as realistically as possible. Each Octagrid (practice) chapter begins with the reasons for making a change and ends with learning points, hints and tips. These chapters provide checklists and lessons learned, which can be transposed to the real environment.

Having followed an Octagrid project, where all three approaches work together, a detailed roadmap for combining the three approaches is presented in Chapter 11. The roadmap is new, simple and appropriate, whatever the order of implementation.

Finally, the publication presents four attributed case studies, in which we see how real companies have adopted some, or all, of the approaches.

The sequence of the publication may seem a little unusual. Within the first six chapters, the practical experiences are presented before the pure description of each approach. This is deliberately done to try to convey something of the different cultures of the approaches, before the reader becomes immersed in the detail. If you prefer the theory first, you may wish to read the first six chapters in the order 2, 1, 4, 3, 6, 5.

The publication consists of 12 chapters:

- Chapter 1 (practice) – Octagrid adopts ITIL
- Chapter 2 (theory) – a concise summary of the main elements of ITIL
- Chapter 3 (practice) – Octagrid uses PRINCE2

- Chapter 4 (theory) – a concise summary of the main elements of PRINCE2
- Chapter 5 (practice) – Octagrid embraces DSDM Atern
- Chapter 6 (theory) – a concise summary of the main elements of DSDM Atern
- Chapter 7 (practice) – Octagrid embarks on a project using all three approaches together
- Chapter 8 (practice) – the combined project is run
- Chapter 9 (practice) – the combined project delivers successfully
- Chapter 10 (practice) – the newly created service is transferred into live operation
- Chapter 11 (theory) – a step-by-step roadmap for a combined project
- Chapter 12 (case studies) – real company case studies from:
  - A private-sector, commercial organization
  - A charity
  - A local authority
  - A national government organization.

MATURITY LEVEL

If you're considering implementing or improving your project management and service management approaches, this publication provides valuable guidance. It attempts to give enough detail of each approach to allow it to be understood by a reader who has overview knowledge of the approaches. However, you should refer to the PRINCE2, ITIL and DSDM Atern official manuals for detailed explanations of the individual approaches.

HOW TO READ THIS PUBLICATION

The publication can, of course, be read sequentially. However:

- If you know any of the approaches in detail, the theory chapter for that approach could be skipped.
- If you do not know any one of the approaches, it may be useful to read the theory chapter for that first, or at least before the Octagrid chapter that looks at the approach in use.
- If you know all of the approaches well, in both theory and practice, the roadmap in Chapter 11, plus the case studies in Chapter 12, will be the most useful. However, you will also find it helpful to refer back to the hints and tips in each of the designated 'practice' chapters.

Whichever way you choose to read this publication, the author hopes that you will find it both enjoyable and helpful.

The calm before
the storm

1

1   The calm before the storm

This chapter covers the first stage of Octagrid's journey: the implementation of ITIL.

In this chapter, you will learn:

- Why the company decided to adopt ITIL guidance
- The strengths of ITIL
- Problems that can occur in the use of ITIL, some of which PRINCE2 and DSDM Atern will address.

1.1   OCTAGRID

Octagrid is a consultancy and software tools company based in the United Kingdom. It has 50 permanent staff and a network of more than 200 consultants worldwide. The consultants are self-employed associates of Octagrid.

The customers of Octagrid's IT services are:

- The network of associate consultants
- Customer companies who have bought the software tools
- Internal human resources, finance and other administrative departments.

Octagrid is growing rapidly and has recently moved to a smart new location, with three storeys of sparkling, glass-sided modern offices and a convenient, secure basement for housing the IT infrastructure. The company is very reliant on its considerable IT investment. However, without formalized procedures to manage or improve it, the IT service was reaching breaking point. As a result, Octagrid has just implemented ITIL. And so the story begins.

1.2   IMPROVING SERVICE MANAGEMENT PROCESSES

1.2.1   What is ITIL?

ITIL is a best-practice approach, which gives guidance on the definition and enhancement of service management processes. It is concerned with managing an organization's IT infrastructure (hardware, software, networks and applications) and providing services based on these to the organization's internal or external customers. Chapter 2 gives a summary of the theory of ITIL and Figure 1.1 is a schematic of the key elements under the control of ITIL.

1.2.2   Why did Octagrid choose ITIL?

For some companies, a corporate risk assessment highlights their dependence on IT services. Octagrid's dependence on its IT services was demonstrated when a router in the basement suddenly failed and, for undiscovered but possibly related technical reasons, the email server was unavailable for three days. As a result the help desk (now the service desk) could not operate, the software tools customers were without support for three days and the consultancy business ground to a halt, causing an unquantifiable but potentially large loss of revenue. Senior management had an uncomfortable practical demonstration of its dependence on IT services. The chief information officer (CIO) insisted that the risk be mitigated and a more professional approach taken to the management of the whole IT infrastructure.

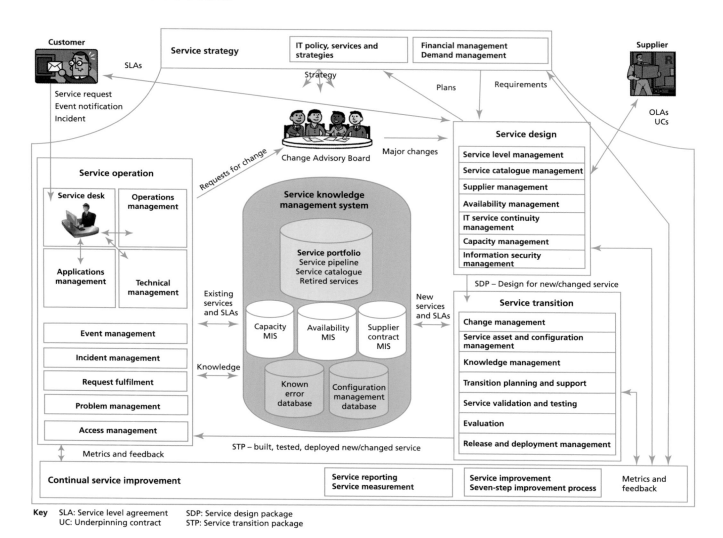

Figure 1.1 The ITIL world

The CIO's stated objectives for implementing ITIL were:

- To be less consumed with firefighting and troubleshooting, and become more proactive
- To consistently serve the real needs of customers
- To be able to work better with suppliers

- To understand the total cost of ownership of IT services across the whole lifecycle of a service.

Everyone in the maintenance and support department received ITIL Foundation training and guidance was sought from a consultant who had already been through ITIL adoption. Octagrid then began its ITIL implementation project by setting out the service management strategy.

1.2.3 The service management strategy

The management reaffirmed the corporate mission: 'To be the best and biggest small IT consultancy, coaching and tools company in the world.'

The 'small' part of this mission reflects the company founders' desire to remain a virtual company, with a small administrative head office and a diverse team of specialist consultants, supported by advanced technology. Remote access to corporate networks was used by consultants all over the world. IT service continuity and server security were recognized as vital. Capacity requirements were hard to predict; availability needed to be close to 24/7/365 because consultants worked all over the world in multiple time zones.

Looking at the business strategy helped focus the purpose and sequence of ITIL adoption. Octagrid used the four Ps from ITIL's *Service Strategy* (TSO, 2007) to outline its IT strategy:

- **Perspective** 'Octagrid will provide market-leading tools, support for tools customers, and good quality, appropriate and available support for its network of consultants.'
- **Position** (based on utility and warranty) 'We will provide market-leading tools and support to our customers and reliable, cost-effective knowledge support to our consultants.'
- **Plan** 'We have set out a detailed plan of the order in which our service management vision will be achieved. We will move from the 'as is' to a desired 'to be' situation in small steps over the next five years, starting from a customer perspective, and focusing first on the areas of greatest pain or current risk. We will treat this

as a major programme of work.'
- **Pattern** 'Our fundamental way of doing things is to offer a dependable, high-quality, high-warranty (availability) service at all times.'

Octagrid identified itself as a Type III service provider (external) to its tools customers and a Type I service provider (internal) to its associate consultants and internal administrative staff.

1.2.4 The implementation plan

ITIL is too big a project to introduce all at once, and the culture change requires time. Typically, medium-sized companies take about 18 months to introduce and adopt all areas of the ITIL guidance. The management of Octagrid decided where to start by asking:

- What are the business objectives?
- Where is the greatest value to be gained?
- Where is our current greatest pain?

As a result of its answers to these questions, Octagrid adopted a customer focus, rather than looking from the inside of IT services, which it might otherwise have been tempted to do.

The implementation began with an assessment of the organization's business needs, and plans were drawn up to use ITIL guidance to address those needs. Major streams of activity for implementation were set up, as shown in Table 1.1. These have now become the streams of work for business-as-usual operations.

Table 1.1 Streams of combined activity for service management process improvement

ITIL process area	Key deliverables
SERVICE STRATEGY	
Strategy generation	Service strategy
Financial management	Service costing and budgeting/change budget control
Business relationship management	Business relationship manager for a service or group of services
SERVICE DESIGN	
Availability management	Business continuity management plan, IT service continuity
IT service continuity management	management plan, availability metrics agreed with the business
Information security management	Services implemented in line with security policy
Capacity management and demand management	Capacity plan for new, changed and existing services
Service portfolio/catalogue management	Service portfolio report
Service level management	Service level agreements
Supplier management	Underpinning contracts
SERVICE TRANSITION	
Change management	Requests for change, forward schedule of change
Release and deployment management, transition planning and support	Implementation plan, release management (or 'go-live') checklist
Service validation and testing/evaluation	Test plans/testing results
Knowledge management	Known error database
Service asset and configuration management	Configuration management database
SERVICE OPERATION	
Incident management/service desk/event management/request fulfilment	Service desk, support and incident resolution groups, service brochure
Problem management	Known error database, requests for change
Operations management/access management/technical management/applications management	Physical infrastructure Operating software Applications software
CONTINUAL SERVICE IMPROVEMENT	
CSI/service reporting/service measurement	Service portfolio report Business questions for continual service improvement

1.3 WHAT WENT WELL

The following worked well for the Octagrid staff during the implementation of ITIL:

- **Strategy first** They asked why they were doing this and focused on the business benefits to be gained. They also set up metrics for the 'as is' situation, to compare at a later date with the 'to be' scenario.
- **Risk** They ran the ITIL introduction as a project and created a business case. They identified risks and options (including the risks and benefits of the 'do nothing' option) and quantified how much reliance the company had on its IT services.
- **The profile of usage** They had previously treated all calls to the help desk (service desk) in the same way. Now with the identification of three different types of customer, each with a very different perception of the value of the services received, they were able to gather data on usage and change the profile of the services offered to suit the different customer types.
- **Incidents and problems** They benefited from the separation of incident management from problem management and the recognition of the different objectives of these two activities: incident – to get the customer up and running as soon as possible; problem – to look for the root cause and fix it, maybe raising a change project in order to do this. This improved customer perception of the service because downtime was shorter, even when the problem itself had not always been solved. A known error database and the logging and traceability of incidents also proved invaluable, in spite of early operator objections to the extra work of logging everything. Tool support also helped immensely.
- **The value held in IT services** Prior to the adoption of ITIL, Octagrid had not had a clear and visible service portfolio or any formal cross-charging of the IT service, internally or externally. Octagrid staff decided not to adopt this fully in Phase 1 but to put in place the means for charging, without actually intending to cross-charge until the profiles of charges that would have been made had been analysed. They were advised that when charging is first set up, charges often emerge that are disproportionate to their value. A prior analysis of charging patterns would allow the identification and removal of anomalies and a fairer charging system to be implemented.

1.4 LESSONS LEARNED

The staff at Octagrid learned many lessons during the implementation process, and the following advice may help others in a similar situation:

- Link the adoption of ITIL guidance to business strategy and treat it as a major organizational change programme. Implementation of ITIL requires significant changes to people's behaviour and jobs. It's important to know what benefits you expect to achieve and not to embark on change just to gain an accreditation (ISO 20000, for example).
- Communicate. Tell people why it matters and tell them over and over in different ways. Much of the opposition to introducing ITIL stems from the fear of change and a lack of understanding about how it will improve life for individual members of staff. A major additional stream of Octagrid's ITIL adoption programme was the communication stream. The ITIL implementation team communicated with Octagrid staff by:

- Using intranet space for frequently asked questions
- Running mini-roadshows face-to-face, by video conference and by webcast, to outline the plans
- Providing named individuals who could be approached with concerns and ideas
- Using posters, newsletters, lunchtime simulations and dramatized presentations.

■ Tell people what it will mean for them and acknowledge both the benefits and the pain in getting there. People's jobs will change and may become more difficult and slower in some cases, and those that immediately benefit may not be the ones that feel the most pain. Automation can help with overheads, but processes have to be clarified first.

■ Carry out stakeholder analysis. Stakeholders are the victims and beneficiaries of change. Communicate continually and clearly with all stakeholders (not just internal ones) at the appropriate level. Stakeholder analysis early on in the project should identify the needs, power and interest of different stakeholder groups.

■ Plan implementation from a customer-facing perspective. The natural inclination is to set up the internal structures first, such as the service asset and configuration management databases. However, a customer focus allows key business benefits to be gained early and improved customer perception leads to customer buy-in. Early visible benefits also help to 'sell' the complex and lengthy change programme to staff.

■ Plan the implementation to solve known pain. Discover what people perceive to be the problems of current operations and target these early. Staff will be more ready to work with the implementation team if they see their problems being addressed.

■ Get skilled help. Octagrid saved itself unnecessary work and stress by consulting an external expert.

■ Foundation training is not enough. Giving everyone ITIL Foundation training establishes a common vocabulary. However, those with responsibility for key areas such as service operations, service desk management, availability and capacity management should attend more in-depth Practitioner courses.

■ Automate service management. For many, the logging and administrative aspects of ITIL represent extra work: everything seems to be more bureaucratic and to take more time. One of the reasons for these negative perceptions is that the person who benefits from this extra information is often a different person from the one doing all the work. Automation helps immensely – provided that it is underpinned by good standards. It is also imperative that measurement and data capture is not excessive. The seven-step improvement process in *Continual Service Improvement* (TSO, 2007) advises: 'Define what you can measure; define what you should measure.'

■ Establish clear baselines before commencing the change programme so that improvements can be measured as soon as they begin to emerge.

■ Give the implementation project/programme a name. This allows people to identify with it better and will help communication.

1.5 PROBLEMS THAT PRINCE2 AND DSDM ATERN MAY ADDRESS

The following quotes from Octagrid service management staff highlight project-related problems, which will be addressed later in this publication:

■ 'There is little or no overlap of knowledge between the ITIL staff, located in the basement at Octagrid, and the new developments department on the second floor. The new developments department has process analysts, business analysts, project managers and developers – as does service design. We're on different floors physically and, culturally, on a different planet!' (service design).

■ 'The new developments department tells release management, just a few weeks ahead of its promised go-live date, that it is ready to put something live. It keeps missing deadlines and then the actual release date comes as a surprise. It may then not be convenient for us to release because of other releases we have planned' (service transition).

■ 'We are skilled in leading change and avoiding 'employee shock'. New development projects take no account of this' (service transition).

■ 'The product that the new developments department thinks is ready to go live is not accompanied by the documentation we need to support it; service desk staff need training to support new products' (service operation).

■ 'It's our job in service transition to perform multiple levels of testing. Even a 'tried-and-tested' package from an external supplier needs considerable work to implement' (service transition).

■ 'The conventions used by the new application may conflict with those of other applications because we were not properly involved in the design' (service design).

■ 'There may not be sufficient capacity to run the new product in the live environment' (capacity management).

■ 'Availability requirements are not specified or are completely unrealistic' (service level management).

■ 'Security may not be properly built in' (information security management).

■ 'No fallback and recovery procedures have been specified' (service transition).

■ 'The business relationship manager has not been involved in the project from the start and has not been involved with service level agreements' (service strategy).

■ 'The artefacts transferred to configuration management are not clear and we have to spend considerable time renumbering them to our conventions' (service asset and configuration management).

These problems arise because service management staff are not properly involved in change projects, and staff in the new developments department do not understand the service management roles, responsibilities and structures.

1.6 CONCLUSION

In this chapter we have discovered why Octagrid adopted ITIL for its service management process improvement, the benefits it realized as a result and the lessons it learned. We have experienced the disconnection between the service management and new development project worlds, and the issues raised will be picked up for discussion later in this publication.

The next chapter is a theory chapter, refreshing the key features of ITIL. In Chapter 3, we return to Octagrid, moving from a dark basement, where the service management and service desk staff are housed, alongside the server rooms, and up to the second floor and the golden world of new development projects. The service desk staff frequently complain, 'We're down here in the dungeon with no windows. Those folks in the new developments department are treated like royalty. We get all the complaints and problems; they get all the fun and a view of the hills!'

Surely only Octagrid would value its service management assets so poorly!

The IT service management landscape

2

2 The IT service management landscape

In this chapter we will look at:

- What service management is
- What a service is
- ITIL version 3:
  - Where ITIL has its roots
  - The ITIL service management lifecycle
  - The structure of ITIL:
    - The five disciplines
    - Processes
    - Roles involved
  - Benefits
  - Risks.

2.1 INTRODUCTION TO THE THEORY

This is the first of three 'theory' chapters, which describe ITIL, PRINCE2 and DSDM Atern in turn. Each is intended as a reference and these quick summaries of the methods will give context to the advice, guidance and references made elsewhere in the publication. Each of these industry best-practice approaches has its own manuals, along with excellent repositories of information and guidance. This, and the other theory chapters, assumes that the reader has some level of knowledge of the approaches. If you are an ITIL service manager, with ITIL version 3 knowledge, you may wish to skip this chapter, and resume the treasure hunt at Chapter 3.

2.2 WHAT ARE ITIL AND SERVICE MANAGEMENT?

ITIL (the Information Technology Infrastructure Library) is a public domain framework for managing the provision of IT services. Refined over many years, ITIL is now the most widely accepted approach to IT service management worldwide.

Published on behalf of the UK Office of Government Commerce (OGC), ITIL first appeared in 1989. A second version was released in 2000, with further supporting publications released over subsequent years. In 2007 this body of knowledge was restructured and ITIL version 3 was born, consisting of five core publications covering the whole service lifecycle, and an introductory guide. It is ITIL version 3 that is outlined here.

Many organizations investing in ITIL are large organizations, e.g. banks, local authorities and airlines. However, organizations of all sizes can benefit from ITIL, whatever their technology platform. ITIL can be tailored to meet the needs of each organization. The case studies in Chapter 12 show a cross-section of organizations, both large and small.

2.2.1 The objective of service management

The primary objective of IT service management is to ensure that IT services provide value for both the customer and the supplier. IT services underpin the business processes and must also act as an agent for change.

2.2.2 What is a service?

The ITIL glossary defines a service as, 'A means of delivering value to customers by facilitating outcomes customers want to achieve without the ownership of specific costs and risks.'

IT services are vital organizational assets. It is essential that these services are managed effectively to deliver value to the business.

When customers buy products or services, they actually buy the satisfaction of a need. The value of the service to the customer is directly dependent on how well it is perceived to address that need. The value of a service depends on both measurable business outcomes and customer perception. Value is a combination of utility (fitness for purpose) and warranty (fitness for use, e.g. availability, reliability, security).

A service is governed by a combination of:

- Service level agreements (SLAs) between the customer and the IT service supplier
- Operational level agreements (OLAs) between the IT service supplier and the internal support teams
- Underpinning contracts (UCs) between the customer and an external supplier.

2.2.3 What is service management?

The ITIL glossary defines service management as 'a set of specialized organizational capabilities for providing value to customers in the form of services.'

ITIL service management covers the whole lifecycle of a service, from the original idea or need, through strategy, planning and design, delivery into operational use, and improvement over time – until the service is finally withdrawn. It also covers the service management process itself.

2.3 THE ITIL SERVICE LIFECYCLE

ITIL v3 covers the five disciplines of the service management lifecycle (as shown in Figure 2.1):

- Service strategy
- Service design
- Service transition
- Service operation
- Continual service improvement.

Service strategy guides each of the other disciplines of service management (Figure 2.2).

Within each lifecycle stage, ITIL defines key processes, roles and main documents/information stores. These are explained in more detail in the rest of this chapter. Figure 2.2 shows the lifecycle phases and the processes within them.

2.3.1 Service strategy

The purpose of service strategy is to encourage a clear business perspective for the development of the IT service management function and the provision of services. A successful service must deliver sufficient perceived value to the customer whilst also giving appropriate reward to the service provider.

There are three different types of service provider:

- **Type I** Internal (embedded within the business function it serves)
- **Type II** Shared service unit (within the customer organization, providing services to many departments – for example, an internal IT department)
- **Type III** External (external to the customer organization, providing services to potentially many customers – for example, a website-hosting service).

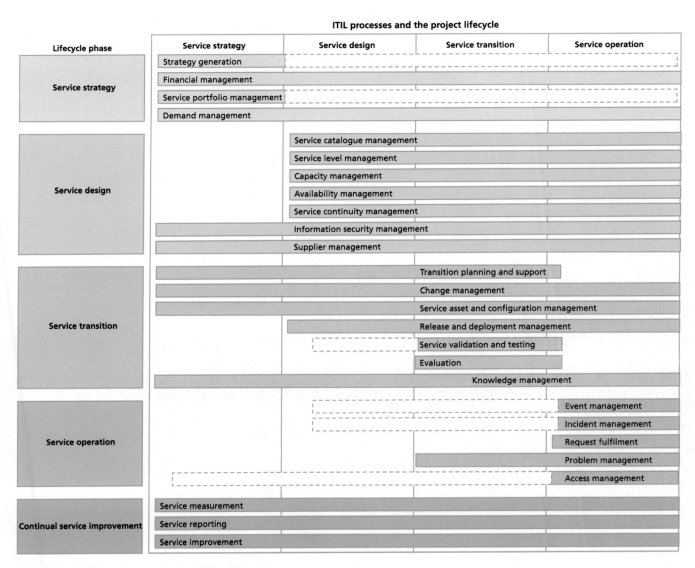

Figure 2.1 Lifecycle coverage of the ITIL processes

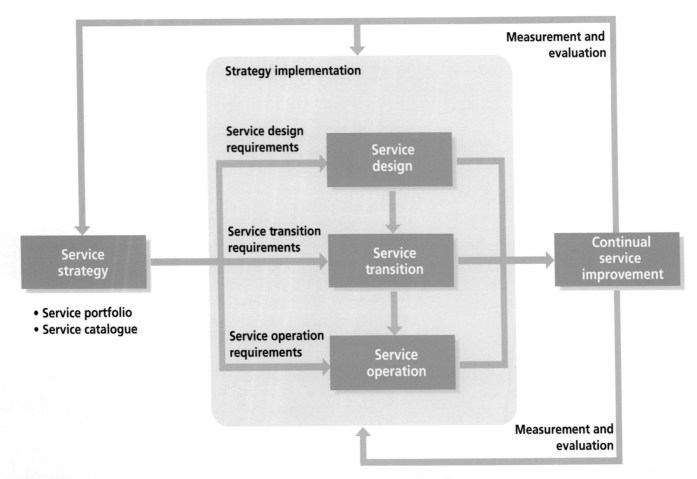

Figure 2.2 How service strategy links to other service management disciplines

The service provider is always in a competitive environment – even the customer with an internal IT department can (and often does) go elsewhere for their IT services. Therefore, the service provider must be able to clearly differentiate its services from the competition.

2.3.1.1 Processes

The processes of service strategy are:

- ■ **Strategy generation** This involves the definition of business requirements, determination of the market space and definition of IT policies and strategies.
- ■ **Financial management** The service provider's budgeting, accounting and charging requirements (the chart of accounts/cost model) are defined by financial management.

- **Service portfolio management** This manages the complete set of services across the service lifecycle. This includes services in concept, design and development stages (service pipeline); live, available services (service catalogue) and retired services.
- **Demand management** As well as monitoring and influencing customer demand for services, demand management also provides the capacity to meet those demands, in conjunction with capacity management.

2.3.1.2 Outputs

The outputs of service strategy are:

- A service level package (incorporating a design for a new or changed service)
- Service design requirements (strategic)
- Service transition requirements (strategic)
- Service operation requirements (strategic).

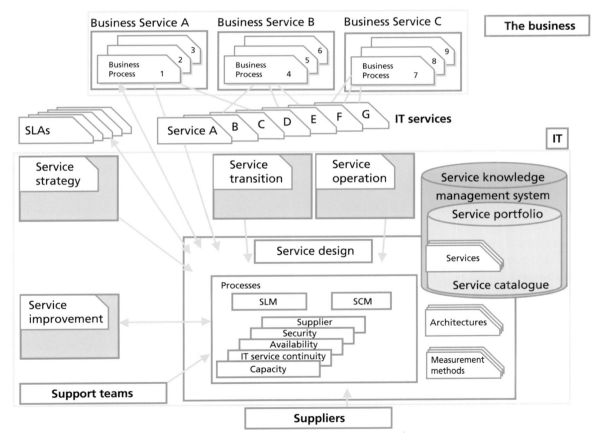

Figure 2.3 The scope of service design

2.3.2 Service design

Service design covers the design of specific new IT services and the design of the service management process itself.

Service design may be triggered by service strategy or by a request for change from a customer, which is approved by the Change Advisory Board. The output is a service design package (SDP), which defines all aspects of the new/changed IT service. The SDP is passed to service transition as a specification against which to test, evaluate and deploy. Service design is a part of the organization's overall business change process. Figure 2.3 shows the scope of service design.

2.3.2.1 Processes

The processes of service design are outlined here. Some processes also have an impact across other lifecycle stages.

- **Service level management** manages the relationship with customers. This involves negotiating service level agreements (SLAs) and monitoring performance against targets for these.
- **Service catalogue management** manages the service catalogue, as the definitive source of information on IT services.
- **Capacity management** is responsible for providing and tuning service capacity to meet agreed current and future business needs. This capacity includes all IT resources.
- **Availability management** provides a point of focus for all availability-related issues across the service lifecycle. It must ensure current and future availability targets are met or exceeded.
- **IT service continuity management (ITSCM)** plans for IT service continuity and recovery, in line with the organization's wider business continuity plan.
- **Information security management** promotes effective information security across all service management activities, in line with wider business security.
- **Supplier management** works closely with the service level manager to negotiate supplier contracts, and ensure that suppliers meet performance targets.

Service design also describes the activities of data management and requirements engineering. It states the aim to select standard, packaged solutions where possible. In addition, there is guidance on application management – the managing of software services throughout their lives.

Interestingly, when service design lists the application management stages, it omits the 'build' stage. **This is ITIL's interface with the project world of application development covered by PRINCE2 and DSDM Atern.**

2.3.2.2 Outputs

The output of service design is the SDP – a blueprint of the design for a new or changed service.

2.3.3 Service transition

Service transition takes a design from service design and converts it into a 'live' service, to be operated by service operation. Service transition also provides early life support for services in operational use, before full handover to service operation. As shown in Figure 2.4, service transition does not actually build the software that forms the applications, but takes responsibility for extensive testing, particularly of non-functional aspects.

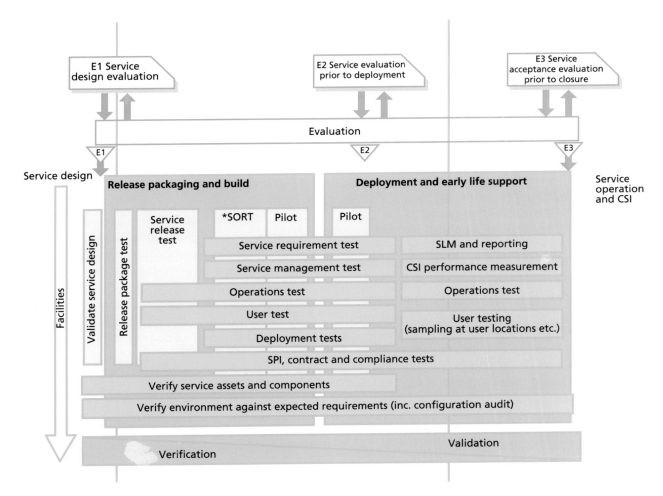

*Service operational readiness test

Figure 2.4 The scope of service transition

2.3.3.1 Processes

The processes marked 'G' (for 'global') have an impact across the whole service lifecycle, not just during service transition:

■ **Change management (G)** provides the mechanisms and standards by which proposed changes to services are evaluated, recorded, authorized and prioritized. Changes are managed through the Change Advisory Board (CAB) and the Emergency Change Advisory Board (ECAB).

■ **Service asset and configuration management (G)** works closely with change management to record, manage and control all service assets.

- **Knowledge management (G)** allows authorized people to obtain appropriate and timely information and knowledge to enable them to deliver and support the services.
- **Transition planning and support** plans and coordinates service transition activities and resources across all projects, teams and services in order to establish new and changed services into service operation in a cost-effective and timely manner.
- **Release and deployment management** assembles the new and changed services and implements these into operational use. This process spans from transition planning through to early life support of the service and handover to service operation.
- **Service validation and testing** is responsible for verifying and validating all services before their release into the live environment. It aims to provide objective evidence that the new/changed service supports the business requirements and meets agreed SLAs, utilities and warranties.
- **Evaluation** occurs once the new or changed service has been released into the live environment. It checks that the design, which has been implemented as specified in the SDP, is still appropriate to the business need and performs as expected in the business and operational environments. It also looks at the effectiveness of the service transition approach itself. Evaluation will also monitor the continued relevance of the service by establishing appropriate metrics and measurement techniques for the service in operation.

2.3.3.2 Outputs

The output of service transition is the service transition package – this incorporates everything needed for the completed release and handover of a service to service operation.

2.3.4 Service operation

The purpose of service operation is to provide agreed levels of service to users and customers and to manage the applications, technology and infrastructure that support the delivery of the services. This involves fulfilling user requests for assistance, resolving service failures and carrying out routine tasks to support and maintain the service. Service operation interfaces with many processes elsewhere in the lifecycle (change control, and service asset and configuration management, for example). Service operation has four key functions, in addition to five processes.

2.3.4.1 Service operation functions

The four key functions of service operation are:

- **The service desk** The 'front line' of service operations, the service desk provides a single point of contact for all users of IT services. It deals with incidents, service requests and access requests and provides an interface for all service operation processes and activities.
- **Technical management** Providing technical expertise and resources to manage the IT infrastructure, technical management also helps to design, test, release and improve services (project involvement) and maintain a stable technical infrastructure.

- **Application management**   A similar role to technical management, but with a focus on software applications rather than infrastructure, application management provides expertise and management of software applications throughout their life.
- **IT operations management**   This comprises:
  - IT operations (operation, management and maintenance of the IT infrastructure)
  - Facilities management (data centres, computer rooms and recovery sites).

Figure 2.5 shows service operation in the context of business requirements and all other stages of the service lifecycle. It illustrates that, whilst a design and development project is ongoing, there is involvement from service transition and service operation staff. There is also a warranty period after release, during which both service transition and service operation are involved.

2.3.4.2 Service operation processes

The five processes of service operation are:

- **Event management**   This detects and notifies service operations staff of normal or exception conditions in the IT infrastructure that affect the management of a service. Some of these may be notified automatically; others may be monitored or observed by staff.
- **Incident management**   An incident is an unplanned interruption to an IT service, or a service quality reduction or threat. Incidents are reported to the service desk in the first instance, where they are logged and prioritized. Subsequently, the appropriate specialist teams may be involved.
- **Request fulfilment**   A service request is a call from a user for information or advice, for a standard change, or for access to an IT service. Requests are made to the service desk. The service desk will provide information, log and track requests and fulfil approved requests.
- **Problem management**   This process is usually brought into action, as a result of a recurring incident, to find the underlying cause and, if appropriate, to raise a change request to permanently resolve the problem or minimize the impact of unpreventable incidents.
- **Access management**   This manages confidentiality, availability and integrity of data and intellectual property. It is responsible for providing authorized access to services and preventing non-authorized access.

2.3.4.3 Service operation outputs

The outputs of service operation are:

- The supply of service to the customer
- The resolution of incidents, problems and requests.

2.3.5 Continual service improvement

Continual service improvement (CSI) is concerned with maintaining value for customers through continual evaluation and improvement of the quality of services and the maturity of the organization's service management processes.

Working closely with the business process owners, users and customers, CSI draws on quality management, change management and capability improvement to optimize each stage in the service lifecycle, as well as the current services, processes, activities and technology. Figure 2.6 illustrates CSI's place in the service lifecycle. To be successful, CSI must become a routine activity.

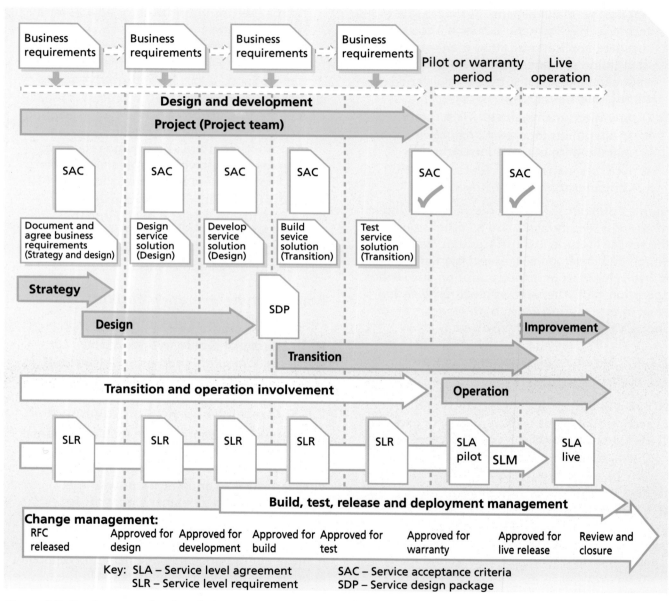

Figure 2.5 Service operation in relation to other service management disciplines

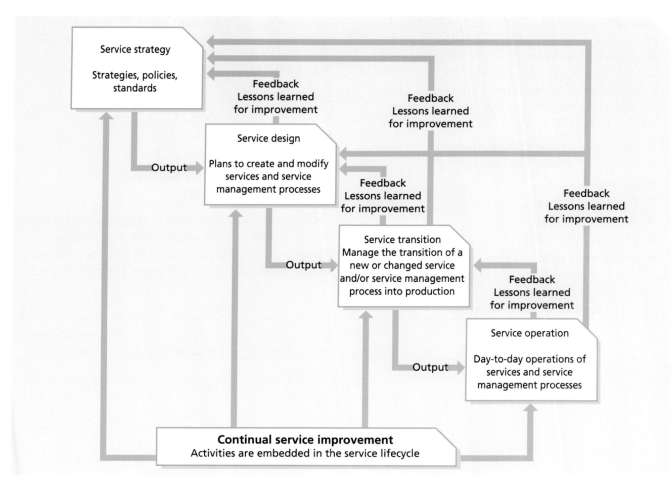

Figure 2.6 CSI and the service lifecycle

2.3.5.1 CSI processes

CSI has three key processes:

■ **Service measurement** In order to allow CSI to function, it is essential that all other lifecycle stages have measurement and reporting embedded within them. Technology, process and service metrics for the end-to-end service may be gathered. Service level management has a key role in this process.

■ **Service reporting** Important aspects of service reporting are identification of the target audience for the report; the purpose and usage of the report; and responsibility for creation and frequency. It is also important that the relevant and useful information that has been produced is appropriately shared and exchanged.

■ **Service improvement**   This follows a seven-step process. The cycle begins with business and IT alignment to identify vision, strategy, and tactical and operational goals. The seven steps below follow on from this. Each step is driven by goals defined during service strategy and service design. The seven steps are:

- Define what you **should** measure
- Define what you **can** measure
- Gather the data
- Process the data
- Analyse the data
- Present information
- Implement corrective action.

The resulting improvement plans are then acted upon.

2.3.5.2 CSI outputs

The outputs of CSI are:

■ Metrics and reports
■ An improvement plan.

2.4   ROLES WITHIN SERVICE MANAGEMENT

Each of the ITIL publications gives guidance on roles and responsibilities. A large number of roles are identified. For reference, some of the key roles are cross-referenced with the lifecycle stages in Table 2.1.

Table 2.1 ITIL roles by lifecycle stage

	Service strategy	Service design	Service transition	Service operation	Continual service improvement
First-level support				X	
Second-level support				X	
Third-level support				X	
Access manager				X	
Account manager	X				
Application developer			X		
Applications analyst/architect		X			
Applications manager				X	
Availability manager		X			
Business analyst		X			
Business relationship manager	X				
Capacity manager	X	X			

	Service strategy	Service design	Service transition	Service operation	Continual service improvement
Change Advisory Board			X	X	
Change manager			X	X	
Change owner			X	X	
Chief sourcing officer	X				
Compliance manager		X			
Configuration manager			X		
Contract manager	X				
CSI manager					X
Customer					X
Director of IT services (SS)	X				
Emergency Change Advisory Board			X		
Financial manager	X				
Incident manager				X	
IT designer/architect		X			
IT facilities manager				X	
IT operations manager				X	
IT operator				X	
IT planner		X			
IT security manager		X			
IT service continuity manager		X			
IT Steering Group	X				
IT strategy manager	X				
Knowledge manager			X		
Major incident team				X	
Problem manager				X	

Table 2.1 ITIL roles by lifecycle stage *continued*

	Service strategy	Service design	Service transition	Service operation	Continual service improvement
Process manager	X				X
Process owner	X		X		X
Product manager	X				
Project manager			X		
Release manager			X		
Risk manager		X			
Service catalogue manager		X			
Service design manager		X			
Service desk manager				X	
Service level manager		X			
Service operation manager				X	
Service owner		X			
Service portfolio manager	X				
Service request fulfilment group				X	
Service transition manager			X		
Supplier manager		X			
Technical/ infrastructure manager				X	
Test manager			X		
User				X	X

2.5 RISKS OF ITIL

Because ITIL is complex:

- The implementation may be too heavyweight, meaning that costs outweigh benefits.
- It may prove to be costly and time-consuming to implement, and implementation may be too patchy for benefits to accrue.
- It may not be seen as good value and may be abandoned before benefits are realized.
- It may not be clear how and where to tailor it, in spite of its emphasis on fit for purpose. Therefore, tailoring may leave out the very elements that would deliver the most value.
- It may not achieve sufficient buy-in from stakeholders.
- IT service management may become disjointed because few people are aware of more than their own ITIL discipline.
- It may restrict creativity and innovation. The very fact that ITIL lays down a framework of business processes may mean that those implementing it do not question these processes and fail to tailor them to the specific needs of the organization.

Because ITIL does not cover the actual building of software:

- There may be confusion about who is responsible for certain processes (for example, testing, training of user staff and operational documentation) with a resulting overlap of effort, or omission of necessary elements.
- The business focus may be on the development project, rather than the ongoing management of the service.
- The service management staff may be brought in to development projects too late, or not at all, resulting in the unknown application being thrown 'over the wall' as an unexpected delivery for a release that service transition and operations are not ready for.

2.6 BENEFITS OF ITIL

Some of the benefits of implementing ITIL include:

- Increased user and customer satisfaction with IT services
- Improved service availability and reduced downtime, directly leading to increased business profits and revenue
- Financial savings from reduced rework, less disruption and loss of productive hours, and improved resource management and usage
- Reduced time to market for new products and services
- Better information for decision making and risk management
- A clear point of contact for customers, leading to perceived easier resolution of problems
- Better information about the total cost of ownership of IT services.

2.7 CONCLUSION

ITIL covers the whole lifecycle of an IT service
– from strategic need, through to design and
transition into a value-adding operational service,
and beyond to the retirement of that service.
Within this lifecycle, many projects may be run to
create or enhance the service. ITIL adds guidance
and structure for the creation and management
of services, but does not define in detail how the
projects within it will be run, leaving this area to
the specialist project management and delivery
frameworks, such as PRINCE2 and DSDM Atern.

Many of the problems with ITIL implementation
relate to the scale of the implementation. If an
incremental, value-focused approach is taken, risks
can be mitigated.

The golden world of
new development
projects

3

3 The golden world of new development projects

Octagrid has just implemented PRINCE2. In this chapter, you will learn:

- Why the company implemented PRINCE2
- What PRINCE2 does well
- Issues that can arise when implementing PRINCE2
- PRINCE2-related problems, which ITIL and DSDM Atern can address.

This chapter rejoins Octagrid in the new developments department on the second floor of its smart new office building. The hills are looking particularly green today. Octagrid is now officially a 'PRINCE2 shop' and the Octagrid project managers have all achieved their PRINCE2 Practitioner status.

Two years ago, the new developments department was in turmoil. It had attempted to develop a basic website, using no formalized project management approach. This endeavour ran seriously over time and budget. Management decided that a new approach to controlling projects was needed.

Octagrid has since implemented PRINCE2 and has also just completed a pilot project (Phase 2 of the web project), using PRINCE2. We shall look at the lessons learned from both the implementation of PRINCE2 and the running of the pilot project.

3.1 THE PRINCE2 IMPLEMENTATION

The management team chose PRINCE2, the UK de facto standard project management approach, because it had a clear framework, management decision points, defined roles and responsibilities, and also 'management by exception', which was particularly appealing to the busy senior managers. Some believed that this meant that project sponsors and senior management would not have to get involved in the projects unless they went into exception – a misunderstanding that had to be corrected!

The reasons why Octagrid felt the need for a project management approach are common to many organizations. They include:

- A lack of clarity of roles and responsibilities, causing individuals and teams to work inefficiently and the wrong voices to be heard during decision making
- A lack of leadership from project managers
- Projects running over time and budget; deadlines being missed and morale falling
- A lack of sustained senior management commitment
- Unclear expectations and acceptance criteria for projects
- No good business case for the project, no clear link to corporate vision or strategy
- No measurement of benefits realized
- Insufficient funding and resources, including resource conflicts with other projects
- No clear visibility of project progress to managers and stakeholders; poor communication
- Risks identified but not managed, so that when they do occur, the organization is unprepared

- Concerns of stakeholders or team members not being addressed; issues remaining unresolved
- Lessons not learned from one project to the next.

3.1.1 The implementation project

Octagrid decided to engage an expert to assist with the implementation project. The PRINCE2 implementation project (P2IMP) was mandated, with the objective of embedding PRINCE2 within the Octagrid culture in a year.

The project board for the implementation project, P2IMP, comprised the CIO as executive, the new developments manager as senior user and the human resources manager as senior supplier – because the human resources manager was the person responsible for procuring the training.

As indicated by the product breakdown structure in Figure 3.1, Octagrid decided on the following major products:

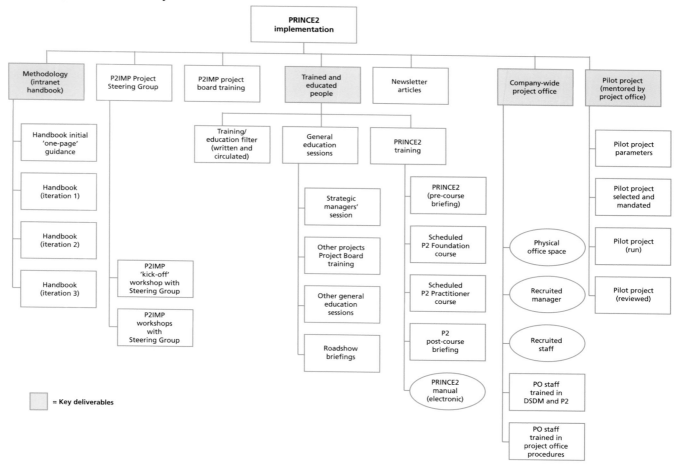

Figure 3.1 Octagrid PRINCE2 implementation project – initial product breakdown structure

- Staff training
- An intranet-based handbook, incorporating advice and templates
- The setting up of a project office
- A pilot project to run with PRINCE2.

The project was deemed successful after one year and formally closed. Although the project office was not fully operational within this time, most of the training had been done, the intranet-based handbook was in place and the pilot project had been completed.

3.1.2 What went well with the implementation project?

Running the PRINCE2 implementation as a project gave a structure to the endeavour and helped to define and control costs. Initially, the human resources manager opposed the idea of a project, insisting that 'a bit of training' was all that was needed. However, the discipline of formulating a business case made the project board focus on what benefits it expected to realize and the costs that were likely to accrue. Drawing a product breakdown structure of the required deliverables made it clear that intranet-based support and the additional training (such as senior management briefings) were needed. The establishment of a project board ensured senior sponsorship of the project.

3.1.3 Lessons learned from the implementation project

Octagrid learned the following lessons during the implementation project:

- The project board needed training in its responsibilities.
- The resources within the project did not

know PRINCE2 from the outset, and some misunderstandings ensued.
- Engaging outside advice from an expert made the implementation project less problematic than it could have been. It also established that not all accredited training is of the same quality.
- The setting up of a project office in the early stages had proved too challenging, until a critical mass of people had received PRINCE2 training. However, this had begun to flourish once the intranet-based handbook had been initiated, and would continue to grow as the number of projects using PRINCE2 increased.

3.2 RUNNING THE PILOT PROJECT

A pilot project ran in parallel with the implementation project. This was Phase 2 of the website project, called WOSP (web ordering system with payments) because of its ordering and e-commerce capabilities.

WOSP was mostly undertaken by internal development staff, although the e-commerce capability was purchased as a customized software package from a local software company.

The project board for WOSP consisted of the CIO as executive, the marketing manager as senior user and the new developments manager as senior supplier. It was thought that the IT services manager was not needed, and this later proved to be a shortcoming. No user or supplier groups were set up – and these would have helped to ensure the right quality of the project deliverables.

The project was not as successful as everyone had hoped, running late throughout and being delayed at implementation by service transition.

3.2.1 What went well with WOSP

The project manager and project board of WOSP agreed that the following points had worked well during the project:

- A formalized, written business case was produced for the first time on a development project. This enabled prioritization of features by business value.
- A clear budget and timeframe were established, with defined management stages for the development. Risks were also assessed at this point, which allowed them to be monitored actively throughout the project.
- The project board established the reporting it required from the project manager. Tolerances were set, which defined the limits of the project manager's authority to vary from the project plan without notifying the project board.
- Work packages and product descriptions were used to control the issue of work to both external suppliers and internal teams, which ensured that work handed out was better specified than in previous projects.
- Quality reviews were run and the creation of product descriptions drove the identification of the right skills to test the products.

3.2.2 Lessons learned from WOSP

Octagrid learned the following lessons during the WOSP project:

- The CIO was too busy to be personally involved for most of the early stages, because the CIO was also the executive for the implementation project. This caused delays in decision making and issue resolution. An executive really does need to be available throughout the project to offer advice and make decisions.
- Most project board decisions were delegated to the senior supplier, who was also the senior user on the implementation project. The overlap of these two new and poorly understood roles caused confusion. More targeted project board training and coaching would have given clarity here.
- The IT services manager should have been involved in the project from the outset, to ensure continuity between the project and service management.
- If user and supplier groups had been set up, this would have helped to ensure the right quality of project deliverables.
- The external suppliers did not know PRINCE2 and failed to appreciate the implications of the late delivery of work packages. Better supplier selection criteria is a future aim.
- The project plan and stage plans were not visible to all stakeholders (the external supplier, for example). This meant that they followed their own plans. Team plans should be created in parallel with stage plans and made visible to all who need them. Checkpoint meetings should be used to assess progress against plans.
- The management stages were too long – by the time it was clear that a stage was behind schedule, it was too late to recover the whole project. Management stages should be shorter, but not so short that they create too great an overhead of stage boundary administration.
- Quality reviews came too late, after the product had been built. As a result, much rework was needed. Quality should be informally reviewed throughout the work package.

3.3 PROBLEMS RELATED TO PROJECT HANDOVER INTO THE LIVE ENVIRONMENT

The project was ready to go live, from the development point of view, only a few weeks later than its original deadline. However, service transition then delayed it for a further two months because:

- Service desk staff were not trained for the new application during the project; more staff needed to be recruited, and service operation had not been involved early enough to anticipate this.
- IT service continuity plans needed to be set up during the project lifecycle, to allow for a smooth handover. IT service continuity management had not been notified and involved during the project.
- Information security management needed to arrange site penetration tests before release, since this was an e-commerce application and a target for hackers. When it received notification of the project, the project was almost complete.
- Capacity management had not been notified at the beginning of the project and, as a result, the extra load on their servers had not been calculated. Demand management had not been considered and peak times would need to be managed.
- Availability management could not guarantee the required availability, which had already been agreed with the customer during the development project.
- Supplier management had not authorized the use of the software package supplier as a service provider. There was no underpinning contract in place for continued support of the packaged elements of the application.

- Service transition insisted on testing the whole application again, even though the development project claimed to have performed extensive testing.
- Service asset and configuration management used different standards for identification of configuration items to those used during the project and required a complete re-identification of all assets.
- Service level management had no SLAs in place, and wanted to negotiate these before release, effectively putting requirements into the project *after* it had been completed!
- Release management had planned a major server upgrade for the same time as the project was due to go live. The project had to wait until that was completed.

3.4 PROBLEMS RELATED TO DEVELOPMENT AND COLLABORATIVE WORKING

The PRINCE2 manual acknowledges that PRINCE2 does not cover:

- The actual development process
- Techniques for team working and collaboration
- Leadership and people-management techniques and approaches.

DSDM Atern will address these areas. It will also address the quality of the developing project, involvement of the right team skills (including service management skills), and the early and incremental delivery of valuable product.

3.5 CONCLUSION

Octagrid now has both ITIL and PRINCE2 in place and has run the pilot PRINCE2 project. It still does not have control over the timely delivery of projects, however, and the interface to service management is awkward. The problems identified here will be addressed in future chapters.

The next chapter is a refresher of the key features of PRINCE2 (2009). In Chapter 5, we explore an agile approach to project delivery, DSDM Atern, which works well alongside both PRINCE2 and ITIL and has the potential to address many of the problems identified in sections 3.3 and 3.4. At Octagrid, this means moving from the second floor of the building in one part of the country to a bunker in a completely different part of the country – a place where they have not yet heard of either PRINCE2 or ITIL!

The project
management
landscape

4

4 The project management landscape

In this theory chapter we will cover:

- PRINCE2 2009:
  - Where project management has its roots
  - What PRINCE2 is
  - Types of PRINCE2 project (not just IT)
  - A summary of PRINCE2:
    - The seven principles
    - The seven themes (including roles and major techniques)
    - The seven processes (the PRINCE2 lifecycle)
  - Benefits
  - Risks.

4.1 INTRODUCTION TO THE THEORY

This chapter summarizes, for reference purposes, the key features of PRINCE2. If you are a PRINCE2 Practitioner, with PRINCE2 (2009) knowledge, you may wish to skip this chapter and make controlled progress to Chapter 5!

4.2 WHAT IS PROJECT MANAGEMENT AND WHAT IS PRINCE2?

4.2.1 What is project management?

Project management is the discipline of planning and organizing work, and managing resources to meet agreed goals and objectives. Projects involve a cross-functional team, brought together for a finite time to address a specific business purpose and produce a particular product or outcome. Two forefathers of project management are Henry Gantt and Henri Fayol. Their work influences the current body of knowledge associated with project and programme management.

4.2.2 What is PRINCE2?

PRINCE2 (PRojects IN Controlled Environments) is a structured project management method, which has become a standard in the UK government and is widely used in all industry sectors, nationally and internationally. PRINCE2 is a non-proprietary method, applicable to all sizes and types of project and based on inputs and experience drawn from thousands of projects.

PRINCE2 is an integrated framework of principles, processes and key themes, with guidance on planning, delegation, monitoring and control of the six key aspects of project performance: cost, timescale, quality, scope, risk and benefit.

PRINCE2 was developed from PROMPTII, created in 1975 by Simpact Systems Ltd and designed originally for software development projects. This was adopted in 1979 by the CCTA (now part of the OGC). It became PRINCE in 1989 and PRINCE2 in 1996. Several updates of the method followed. The summary here is based on a refresh of the method completed in 2009.

PRINCE2 works well with many different development lifecycles. It focuses on governance and controls the project in a series of management stages, with a formal decision point at the end of each stage, at which it is decided whether to continue with the project or to stop. The structure of the method (depicted in Figure 4.1) is described in the following sections.

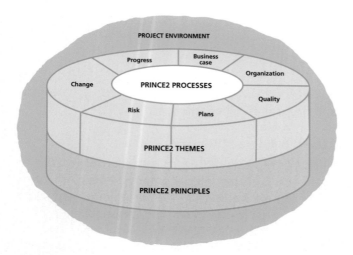

Figure 4.1 The structure of PRINCE2

4.3 THE SEVEN PRINCIPLES

The seven guiding principles originate from lessons learned from a wide variety of projects over time, and they provide a framework of good practice. The PRINCE2 principles are shown in Figure 4.2. They are:

- **Principle 1: Continued business justification**
  A PRINCE2 project must have a sound reason to start, which is agreed, documented and authorized at the outset and kept under review throughout the project. This should be aligned with corporate strategy and documented in an approved business case. If, at any point, the project is no longer justifiable, it should be stopped.

- **Principle 2: Learn from experience**   PRINCE2 project teams are actively encouraged to seek out the lessons learned documented by other projects and also to gather lessons from their own project, throughout the life of that project.

- **Principle 3: Defined roles and responsibilities**   A PRINCE2 project has defined roles and responsibilities for governance and day-to-day management of the project, covering business, user and supplier interests.

- **Principle 4: Manage by stages**   A PRINCE2 project is planned, monitored, controlled and authorized on a stage-by-stage basis. Management stages are sequential and provide control points at which to review plans, re-assess the project against the business case and make the all-important 'go' or 'no-go' decision.

- **Principle 5: Manage by exception**   Managers need to allow people the freedom to work, but without losing control. To achieve this in a PRINCE2 project, each management level sets tolerances against time, cost, quality, scope, risk and benefit. If these tolerances are forecast to be breached at any point during the project, the manager at the level where the deviation has occurred alerts the management level above and requests a decision on how to proceed. This concept is referred to as management by exception.

- **Principle 6: Focus on products**   A PRINCE2 project is product oriented rather than activity oriented. It focuses on delivering products to meet defined, documented quality criteria, and measures progress by completed, approved products.

- **Principle 7: Tailor to suit the project environment**   The PRINCE2 method should be tailored to suit each project. Tailoring, however, does not usually mean omitting elements completely. Rather, the elements of the approach should be adapted to the scale and complexity of the project.

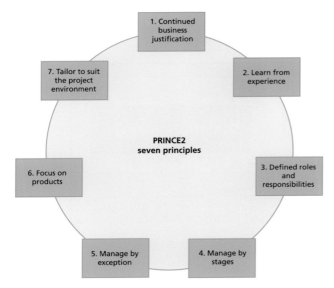

Figure 4.2 The seven PRINCE2 principles

Figure 4.3 The seven PRINCE2 themes

4.4 THE SEVEN PRINCE2 THEMES

The seven PRINCE2 themes (see Figure 4.3) describe key aspects of project management that must be addressed throughout the project:

■ **Theme 1: Business case** A project starts with an idea considered to have potential corporate value. The purpose of the business case is to establish mechanisms and criteria to judge whether the project is, and remains, desirable, viable and achievable. If business justification disappears at any point, the project should be stopped or changed.

■ **Theme 2: Organization** The purpose of the organization theme is to establish the project's structure of accountability and responsibility.

The PRINCE2 organization structure has roles for directing, managing and delivering the project. Each role has a defined set of responsibilities. Some roles may be shared or combined according to the project's needs but the responsibilities must always be allocated and no roles omitted. Figure 4.4 illustrates the organization of roles within a PRINCE2 project.

A PRINCE2 project recognizes three different stakeholder interests: business, user and supplier. All of these must be satisfied if the project is to be successful. Every PRINCE2 project is directed by a project board, which includes representatives from each of these categories.

Project board members are also responsible for project assurance, to ensure that the project is aligned to their respective areas of concern and being managed effectively. A good project board has clear authority, sufficient seniority and credibility. It should have the ability to delegate, but the availability to make decisions and give direction when needed.

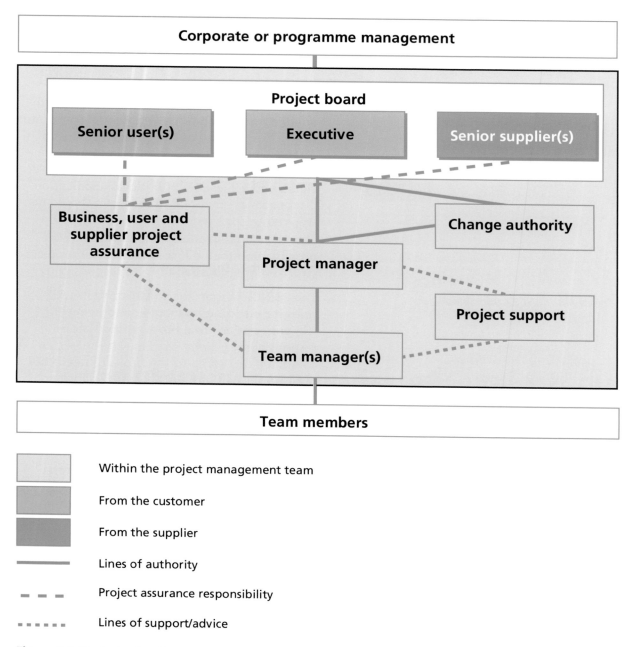

Figure 4.4 Project roles diagram

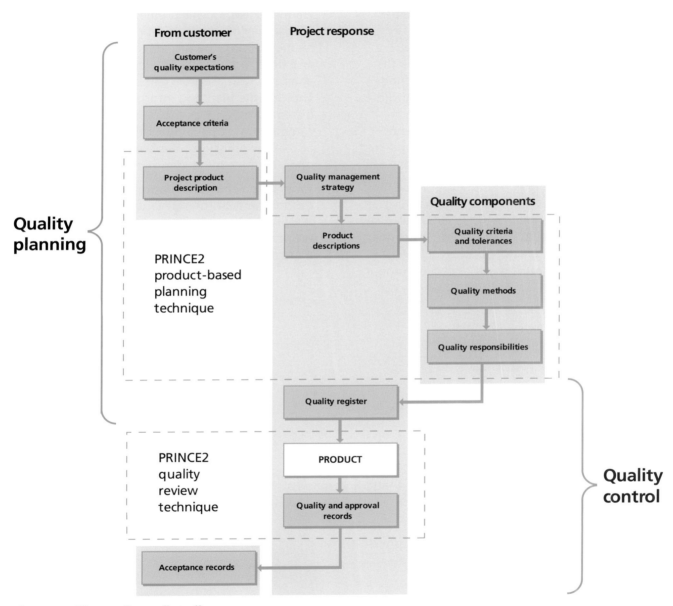

Figure 4.5 The quality audit trail

■ **Theme 3: Quality** The quality theme guides the creation of products that are fit for purpose, i.e. products that meet business expectations and deliver the desired benefits. The theme covers quality standards, methods and responsibilities related to both the project's outcomes and management. It also covers continual improvement of project processes. The PRINCE2 approach to quality is summarized by the quality audit trail shown in Figure 4.5.

One technique for checking quality is the quality review. This is a formalized meeting, with clear roles. Its purpose is to collaboratively identify errors in a product and agree actions to correct these. It is also a powerful way of gaining formal sign-off of an approved product.

■ **Theme 4: Plans** This theme aims to provide a clear way of communicating what *should* happen during the project, including resources and timeframe. Plans provide a baseline against which progress can be measured. They enable planning information to be disseminated to stakeholders in order to secure commitments that support the plan. They also allow omissions, duplication, threats and opportunities to be identified.

Every plan requires the approval and commitment of the relevant levels of the project management team. PRINCE2 recommends three levels of planning, as illustrated in Figure 4.6.

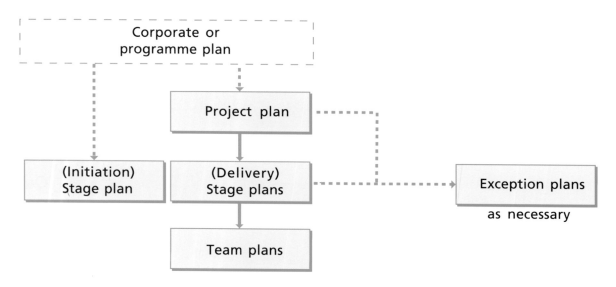

Figure 4.6 PRINCE2 planning levels

PRINCE2 takes a product-based planning approach, before defining activities for the plan. This shows what the project intends to produce and allows progress to be measured by completed products.

■ **Theme 5: Risk**   A risk is an uncertain event (or set of events) that, should it occur, will have an effect on the achievement of the project's objectives. It may be a threat or an opportunity. The risk theme helps to identify, assess and control uncertainty within a project. For risk management to be effective, risks need to be identified, assessed and controlled. The PRINCE2 risk management procedure is shown in Figure 4.7.

■ **Theme 6: Change**   The change theme describes how the changes and issues that occur during the project should be captured, assessed and controlled. It also covers configuration management, which is essential to the effective control of change and issues. An 'issue' is any concern, query, request for change, suggestion or off-specification raised during a project. The issue and change control procedure (see Figure 4.8) ensures that any issues raised or changes requested are assessed and then formally approved, rejected or deferred.

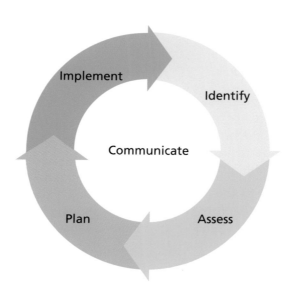

Figure 4.7 The PRINCE2 risk management procedure

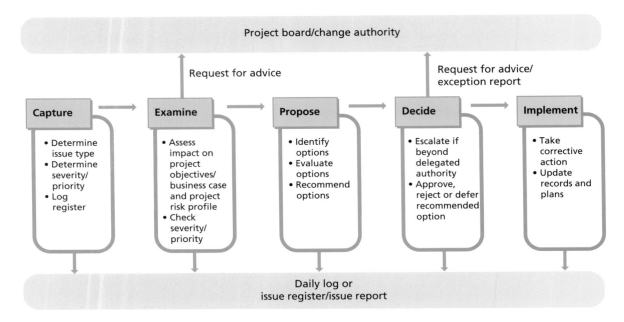

Figure 4.8 Issue and change control procedure

Configuration management is concerned with controlling the creation, maintenance and change of products throughout the project, and the handover to the system under which it will be managed for the lifetime of the product.

■ **Theme 7: Progress** The purpose of the progress theme is to establish mechanisms to monitor and compare achievements against the plan, and to provide a forecast for the project's continued viability whilst controlling any unacceptable deviations from the plan (exceptions).

Control of progress is about ensuring that the project remains viable against its approved business case.

4.5 THE PRINCE2 PROCESSES

The seven PRINCE2 processes and the relationships between the processes are shown in Figure 4.9. They are not necessarily sequential: Directing a Project happens in parallel with other processes; Controlling a Stage, Managing a Stage Boundary and Managing Product Delivery may happen several times during a project. The seven processes are:

■ **Starting up a Project** Starting up a Project gains approval for the initiation of a project and prevents unjustifiable projects from being initiated. The process should be short. The aim is to do the minimum necessary to enable the decision to initiate the project and to put in place prerequisites for Initiating a Project. It ensures that key roles and responsibilities are assigned and that the work required for project initiation is planned.

■ **Directing a Project** This process structures the project board's involvement in the project, allowing it to be accountable for the project's success by making key decisions and exercising overall control at appropriate points, whilst delegating day-to-day management of the project to the project manager.

■ **Initiating a Project** This establishes a sound basis for the project and a common understanding, between stakeholders, of the reasons for the project: its scope, plans, costs, benefits expected and associated risks. It sets up roles and responsibilities for the project and strategies for quality, configuration management, testing, project control and

communication. It also determines how PRINCE2 will be tailored to the project.

■ **Controlling a Stage** Controlling a Stage covers project progress during each management stage. Its purpose is to provide the project manager with a mechanism for assigning work to teams (work packages), monitoring this work, dealing with issues and risks, reporting progress to the project board and taking corrective action to ensure that the stage remains within tolerance.

■ **Managing Product Delivery** This process establishes the link between the project manager and the team manager(s) to allocate and accept work to be done. It places formal

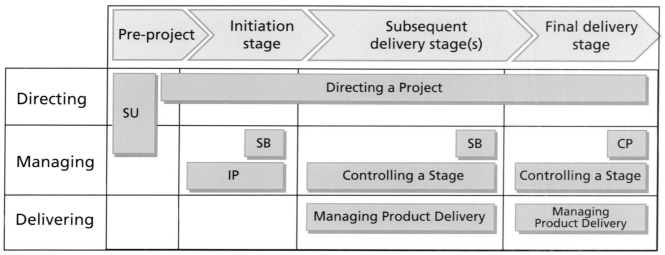

Key
SU = Starting up a Project
IP = Initiating a Project
SB = Managing a Stage Boundary
CP = Closing a Project

Note
• Starting up a Project is used by both the directing and managing levels.
• There should be at least two management stages, the first of which is the initiation stage.
• Managing a Stage Boundary is first used at the end of the initiation stage and repeated at the end of each subsequent stage except the final stage. It is also used to prepare exception plans, which can be done at any time including in the final stage.
• For complex or lengthy initiations, Controlling a Stage and Managing Product Delivery can optionally be used to manage the initiation stage.

Figure 4.9 The seven PRINCE2 processes

requirements on accepting, executing and delivering project work within tolerance, and reporting back to the project manager at an agreed frequency.

- **Managing a Stage Boundary** Managing a Stage Boundary enables the project manager to provide the project board with sufficient information to review the current stage, approve the next stage and confirm the continued business justification for the project. The process is executed at, or close to, the end of each management stage. It is also used in an exception situation, when tolerances are threatened.
- **Closing a Project** The final process provides a clear end to the project and gives a fixed point for acceptance of the project's products, or closure of a non-viable project. It allows for verification of user acceptance and handover to service management. It prompts a review of the performance of the project itself and assessment of immediate and future benefits of the project's delivered products.

4.6 BENEFITS OF PRINCE2

The key benefits of adopting PRINCE2 are:

- It reduces project risk by providing clear governance, a proven process framework and best-practice advice, which has been shown to be effective.
- It can be applied to any project.
- It is easily implemented alongside other specialist, industry-specific development lifecycles.
- It promotes effective communication by providing a common vocabulary for all project participants and a clear, economical approach to reporting.

- It provides a clear structure for accountability, delegation and authority and enables participants to understand their own, and each other's, roles and responsibilities. It ensures that stakeholders are properly represented in planning and decision making.
- Its product focus clarifies what a project will deliver.
- Its plans are designed to meet the needs of the different management levels, improving communication and control.
- It enables management by exception, promoting efficient and economic use of management time at all levels.
- It retains focus on viability throughout the project.
- It promotes learning and continuous improvement of processes.
- It facilitates the assurance and auditing of project work.
- It is well supported by accredited training and expert support.

4.7 RISKS IN THE USE OF PRINCE2

Some of the key risks of using PRINCE2 are listed here, using the PRINCE2 **risk cause**, **risk event** and **risk effect** format:

- The approach is followed without question. This can lead to robotic project management, which may result in poor project outcomes.
- The method is not followed at all. People are under the impression that PRINCE2 is in place, so people attribute poor outcomes to PRINCE2 and reject the method.

- People misinterpret tailoring. Only selected parts of the method are used, losing the integrity of the interconnected nature of PRINCE2 elements, resulting in poor project outcome.
- PRINCE2 is not tailored. The project management effort and approach are not appropriate for the needs and size of the project. The project runs over time and budget, and PRINCE2 is rejected for being too 'heavyweight'.
- PRINCE2 becomes an end in itself. Focus is lost on the need to deliver working, valuable products into the business environment. The project fails.
- Management by exception is misinterpreted. Senior management does not understand the need to give time to the project or blames the project manager for incompetence if it is asked for advice. The project cannot gain the benefits of business focus and delivers the wrong product, or does not deliver.
- PRINCE2 states that the project manager should take care not to deliver beyond the scope agreed. The project environment changes, but the project manager blocks change. The outcome is a product that fits specification but not the business need at the time of delivery.

4.8 CONCLUSION

In this chapter we have looked at the seven principles, seven themes and seven processes of PRINCE2 that provide control and focus for management throughout a project. We have also seen some of the risks and benefits of the approach.

By dividing the project into management stages, PRINCE2 allows control over the release of budget and has clear review points at which progress can be assessed.

The organization of the project management team, the involvement of the right stakeholders within the project board and a clear escalation process for handling issues and changes, predispose towards a project that is effectively managed and controlled, and delivers on time and on budget to meet the business need.

In the next chapter we return to Octagrid, which is planning to try an agile approach, DSDM Atern, to ensure a project is delivered on time.

The deadly
triangle

5

5 The deadly triangle

Having already introduced ITIL and PRINCE2, Octagrid is now looking to adopt DSDM Atern to help it deliver a time-critical project.

In this chapter, you will learn:

- Why Octagrid decided to use DSDM Atern
- What the approach is good at
- Problems that can occur in its use
- Problems that are addressed by using DSDM Atern with PRINCE2 and ITIL
- … and how to turn the deadly triangle on its head!

5.1 INTRODUCTION

The scene unfolds in a dark, cavernous room on an industrial estate. The room has no furniture and two of Octagrid's newest staff, a project manager and a senior IT developer, are standing in the middle of it, surveying the scene:

Developer: 'Why are we in a bunker?'

Project manager: 'It's hardly a bunker, pal. It's a bit grim, I'll admit, but we'll need a room to call our own: a project room, a war room, somewhere to keep the plans visible and where we can meet and really communicate; somewhere we can run facilitated workshops without waiting for days for a free meeting room. This is the only place the management could offer us. Apparently they acquired it some time ago in settlement of a bad debt and have been wondering what to do with it ever since.'

Developer: 'This project, then – bit of a rush job? Is it do-able?'

Project manager: 'Not a chance, mate, if we go for a waterfall approach! We'll have to do a bit of 'agile' or we're out of a job again for sure.'

5.2 THE FIRST DSDM ATERN PROJECT

The marketing director has announced that it is critical to the company's continued viability to build a new software tool for presentation at a trade show in three months' time. The product must be 'awesome', as this trade show is Octagrid's major marketing route for software tools and its reputation will be damaged if it is unable to produce something really innovative. Unfortunately, resources to begin this project could not be found earlier in the year and now the timeframe is too tight. The new developments department has only just been given the mandate for this project and the trade show is in exactly twelve weeks. Will DSDM Atern be able to help?

DSDM Atern is the longest established and certainly most rigorous of the agile approaches. It is the de facto standard for agile in the UK and has very attractive promises for project delivery because it will:

- Deliver on time
- Stay within budget
- Keep management and other stakeholders well informed
- Maintain focus on the business need

■ Deliver regular increments of real business value.

The deadly triangle, also known as the iron triangle, is the project manager's nightmare. Project management has to balance the constraints of cost and time against the features that have to be delivered (see Figure 5.1). If cost, time and features are all fixed, the only dimension left to vary is quality. Compromising quality is an unacceptable outcome. DSDM Atern turns the deadly triangle on its head and advocates fixing quality, along with time and cost, but allows flexibility of scope (features) by prioritization (the MoSCoW rules: **m**ust have, **s**hould have, **c**ould have and **w**on't have this time).

DSDM Atern is rare amongst agile approaches in that it recognizes a project structure and the need for delivery of a clear product to meet a business objective by a definite date and at a definite cost. DSDM Atern will add structure and rigour to a project, without losing the flexibility to adjust to the changing needs of the business.

5.2.1 Why did Octagrid decide on DSDM Atern?

Some of Octagrid's most experienced project managers estimated that at least 15 months would be needed to complete the project. This was unthinkable – creativity was called for. A new project manager was recruited who was not

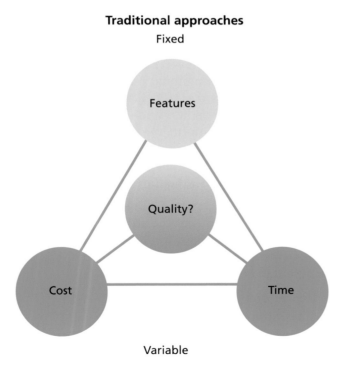

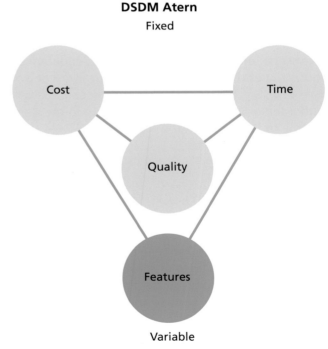

Figure 5.1 The deadly triangle

familiar with PRINCE2, but was a DSDM Atern practitioner and had delivered challenging projects using DSDM Atern for other organizations. The project manager was given a team of six developers and a mission to get something new, useful, working and different from the competition to the trade show, on time.

5.3 DSDM ATERN IMPLEMENTATION

The full implementation of DSDM Atern at Octagrid will have to wait, although there should be an implementation project, and a culture change initiative if the approach is to become properly embedded into the organization's practices. (DSDM Atern has guidance on implementing the approach into an organization.) Octagrid is in a desperate situation. The implementation could be considered to be incremental – it will be used for this one pilot project first and, if successful, will be considered for others.

5.4 THE PILOT PROJECT

The project, PlanBot, will produce an interactive, futuristic work planning and control tool to rival market leaders at a fraction of the cost. It's anticipated that the tool will have hundreds of features, and allow a manager to:

- Enter worker name, location, skills and availability from anywhere in the world
- Enter tasks
- Assign cost and duration to tasks
- Assign tasks to workers
- Amend any data, under privilege security
- Report on who is currently doing each task, which tasks are unassigned and how much of each task has been completed

- Work with the tool in a secure way via the internet and intranet.

We shall follow this project through the phases of the DSDM Atern lifecycle, highlighting key decisions and features of each phase. This is a challenging project and, as with all such projects, the key is a realistic assessment, early on in the project, of what it is actually possible to achieve within the timeframe. This vision also needs to be reaffirmed throughout, and a collaborative approach taken to delivering a fit-for-purpose solution, managing expectations and focusing on a clear, time-bound objective.

5.4.1 Pre-project

A PRINCE2 project mandate was the start point for the 12-week project and meets the required output from a DSDM Atern pre-project phase. This sets out the justification for the next stage of the project to be embarked upon, namely feasibility. It will detail the reason for the project, confirming that it is consistent with the business strategy and putting resources in place to support the feasibility phase.

5.4.2 Feasibility

The first steps were to get sponsorship for the project, a clear objective in business-value terms and the agreement to release the necessary user resources for the duration of the project. Whilst it is not essential for DSDM Atern to have resources dedicated to the project, it shortens timescales considerably and reduces risk to do so. The marketing director agreed to be both business sponsor and business visionary, having had the roles and responsibilities explained. The marketing director assigned the marketing manager as business ambassador, with promised support from a focus group of real end users, who would be available regularly throughout the project.

A kick-off facilitated workshop was organized with key stakeholders to launch the project and establish a clear objective and project vision. A quick but effective business case was also assembled at this workshop. It was recognized that there were actually two objectives: a completed tool, and a product for demonstration of a subset of key features to impress at the trade show. This recognition allowed planning to focus on the second objective, whilst putting in place 'soft' plans for the first.

The project manager and business sponsor reviewed the project approach questionnaire (PAQ) informally, and used the results to establish the best agile working environment they could, given the timeframe.

A feasibility prototype was assembled to clarify the type of interface sought and highlight key attractive features for the final product. The question was raised: 'Could we buy software and customize it?', but this was rejected by the business sponsor as not meeting the vision of an 'awesome' product.

The project manager negotiated a project room (the bunker!) to avoid delays in booking rooms for workshops and to give the developers a place to display plans and keep developing project artefacts visible.

Feasibility lasted just one week. The business sponsor authorized the project to continue.

5.4.3 Foundations

Three workshops were held on consecutive days:

- The first workshop involved key stakeholders and a brief introduction to the DSDM Atern approach, highlighting the concept and implications of MoSCoW prioritization, timeboxing and role responsibilities. A high-level requirements list was elicited and prioritized.
- A second workshop was held to estimate the time needed to meet each requirement, and necessitated a reprioritization of the requirements. The business visionary, business ambassador and solution developers were involved in the estimating to ensure not only accuracy, but also buy-in and commitment.
- Finally, a planning workshop was run, involving the marketing director, marketing manager, project manager and solution developers, to put the prioritized requirements into a timeboxed delivery plan. This workshop also identified risks and mitigations and reaffirmed the business case.

A high-level diagram of the functions of the tool and their interrelationships was a helpful input to these workshops. The delivery plan that emerged was divided into two-week timeboxes, to give a high degree of control.

5.4.4 Exploration and engineering

By week three, the team was ready to work in the development timeboxes shown on the delivery plan, which it now had displayed in large format on the wall of the project room, and which can be seen in outline in Figure 5.2.

The team allowed a one-week 'Timebox 0' at the start of the plan, to establish the development environment and agree standards for working. Beyond this, every timebox had a clearly defined, business-valuable complete feature of the product which it would deliver. Daily stand-ups kept the team apprised of each other's progress and short timeboxes kept up the momentum of delivery.

Some lower-priority elements ('should have' and 'could have' requirements) were allowed time in each timebox in the plan. However, some had to be de-scoped, and these were kept visible on a 'won't have this time' list on the wall of the project room, clearly marked for a next phase of development (whenever that might be). The prioritization workshop ensured that the 'must haves' really

did represent a minimum but valuable subset of features for the trade show.

5.4.5 Deployment

In parallel with the exploration and engineering activity, which was set to regularly deliver finished, tested products, a stream was set up to consider deployment. In the first instance, deployment only focused on delivery to the trade show, and included the production of marketing materials to promote the product.

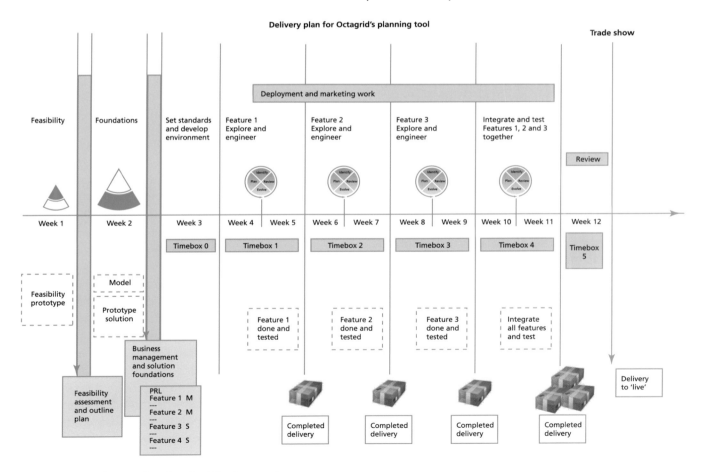

Figure 5.2 Delivery plan for the PlanBot project

5.4.6 Post-project

The post-project phase was not formally run and benefits realization has yet to be assessed. However, the following sections consider what went well and the main learning points.

5.5 WHAT WENT WELL

The good points of the project were:

- It assembled the right user and development resources, owing to the commitment of its strong business sponsor.
- The marketing manager (business ambassador) organized focus groups that brought in representative 'real user' views early on in the project and dispelled misunderstandings about what would be really valuable or impressive to a customer.
- Everyone had clear roles and responsibilities, which avoided confusion and speeded up progress.
- The establishment of a shared vision and objective, plus the business case, focused effort.
- The high-level prioritized requirements were sufficient to steer the work, with more detail being discovered during the development timeboxes. This meant that when requirements were de-scoped, not too much upfront work had been done on them, which would have been wasted.
- Facilitated workshops gained buy-in and commitment, and ensured that good ideas were shared.
- Daily stand-ups were greeted with scepticism at first, as it was thought that they would be time-wasting meetings. However, at only 15 minutes maximum per day, they acted as a motivator, once the tight format was understood by all.
- Displaying the plans on the walls ensured that the current version of the plan was always visible. Everyone could clearly see exactly what they, and everyone else, should be working on.
- Iterative development allowed the team to embrace change and learn as the project progressed. It also allowed for a couple of good ideas, not thought of at the start of the project, to be incorporated in exchange for less useful features.
- When the project did begin to run late, this was evident within a day and could be corrected in the team without recourse to higher management, which would have introduced further delay.

5.6 LESSONS LEARNED

The project did not run perfectly, but it was able to successfully deliver a credible and exciting new product to the trade show by:

- Focusing constantly on the true objective and prioritizing towards this
- Listening to the user input regarding what was really important.

Some lessons learned were:

- Not all of the functionality that the marketing director had imagined was completed in time for the show, but the de-scoping was done visibly and by agreement throughout the project. This meant that expectations were successfully managed.
- The project was successful because the right people were available when needed and everyone was prepared to collaborate and take a realistic attitude to what was possible in the time.

■ There were some misunderstandings about the method, which would have been dispelled by training the whole team (including the business ambassador) from the outset. In retrospect, it would have saved more time than the training would have taken.

■ The expertise for the DSDM Atern approach came from the project manager. However, the project manager was usually too busy to take time out to explain the finer points to the team or to help people customize the process. A separate coaching role would have helped here.

■ Communication was sometimes a problem. Not everyone could work in the project room (marketing, for example, was located in an entirely different region). Thus, communication sometimes suffered – for example, one workshop was completely missed by two members of the focus group because they could not see the plan and had put the wrong dates in their diaries. A visible plan, in an online, web-based collaboration tool, would have helped.

■ A PRINCE2-style communication strategy would have allowed senior management and other stakeholders to be better informed. This would have been even more important on a larger project, with a wider group of stakeholders and several small teams working in parallel.

■ The next phase of development should never be a vague 'whenever that might be' statement. A clear budget for further development would have made prioritization easier in this increment and given confidence of when any requirements de-scoped from this project could be scheduled for development.

5.7 SERVICE MANAGEMENT INTERFACE PROBLEMS

Because the project's increment was a trade show launch, the use of the product in a real environment had not been included in the plans. No service management roles were invited into the project and yet this product would eventually:

■ Have to be supported by the service desk, once people had purchased it. Its supportability and the training of service desk operatives had not been considered.

■ Have to run on Octagrid's own servers. No one had checked with capacity management regarding server capacity, demand management, the effects of possible new hardware acquisition on the pricing of the product, and a tenuous business case.

■ Need to be secure, holding customer-confidential data. Information security had not been involved. Although the first increment did not need this security to be physically there, the involvement of information security could have provided information on security features, to be included in the sales brochures, and integrated into the production version of the tool.

■ Have to be maintainable and offer an appropriate level of availability. Maintainability and availability were low priorities for the release to the trade show, but would have to be built into the production version of the tool, which might fundamentally have affected its design.

5.8 WHAT PROBLEMS DOES OCTAGRID STILL HAVE?

Within Octagrid, there is now expertise in DSDM Atern, PRINCE2 and ITIL, but its project problems are not yet over. In the words of Octagrid's project manager:

We managed to get a credible new product to the show. Now we need to persuade the service management people to support it when it starts making sales. If we had been making releases into an already established live environment, we would not have been able to manage it without service transition support. Also, although the business sponsor fought our corner, we did not seem to inspire management confidence with our apparent informality. If we can engage the PRINCE2 governance roles, I think the management may see we have a lot to offer in the team-control and on-time delivery areas, and a set of useful techniques for collaborative team working. Maybe then we will be allowed out of this bunker!

5.9 CONCLUSION

So we have seen, in overview, how a small DSDM Atern project runs. This was a time-critical situation and was highly valued by some senior managers. However, every project should be important to someone in authority and any late project jeopardizes the meeting of its business case by going over time and budget. Every project should have a sponsor!

If all projects have clear, visible objectives, prioritize what they plan to do from the outset and run in timeboxes, they **will** deliver to plan, or at least there will be very early warning if they are likely not to. If all projects make planned, frequent deliveries, each with real business value, the required return on investment will be realized.

This approach will also scale up to the very largest of projects if the resources are sub-divided into small multi-skilled teams and the features are prioritized and compartmentalized into small cohesive elements that can deliver value early.

The next chapter looks at some of the DSDM Atern theory that underpins this project.

DSDM Atern

6

6 DSDM Atern

In this theory chapter we cover:

- DSDM Atern version 2:
  - What DSDM Atern is
  - Where it came from
  - Types of DSDM Atern project (not just IT)
  - A summary of DSDM Atern:
    - The eight principles
    - Roles and responsibilities
    - The project lifecycle
    - The five key techniques
    - The seven processes
  - Benefits and risks.

6.1 INTRODUCTION

This chapter summarizes, for reference, the key features of DSDM Atern. If you are already a DSDM Atern practitioner, with DSDM Atern version 2 knowledge, you can MoSCoW-prioritize your involvement in this timebox and make an agile leap to Chapter 7!

6.2 WHAT IS DSDM ATERN?

DSDM Atern is an agile project delivery framework for business solutions, created by practitioners and maintained by the DSDM Consortium. It is appropriate for all types of project, not just software development. The approach is free to view and free to use (see www.dsdm.org for full details).

DSDM Atern provides a framework to support the development and deployment of high-speed, high-quality business solutions in increments and within tight timescales. The priority is to deliver business value to the customer on time, in budget and to the right quality – rather than focusing on a fixed, rigid specification. It is essential to understand that if time and cost are fixed, the functionality and features to be delivered must be flexible, otherwise the quality of outcome is jeopardized.

The structure of DSDM Atern is shown in Figure 6.1 (the 'temple' diagram) and comprises:

- The philosophy
- The eight principles
- The process (the lifecycle)
- The people (roles and responsibilities)
- The products (outputs that control the process or represent the project outcome)
- The practices (a set of key agile techniques).

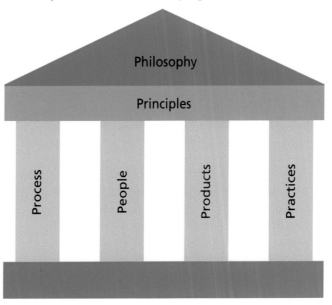

Figure 6.1 The structure of DSDM Atern

The key techniques that DSDM Atern uses to achieve the development and deployment of high-speed, high-quality business solutions in increments and within tight timescales are:

- MoSCoW prioritization
- Facilitated workshops
- Iterative development
- Modelling and prototyping
- Timeboxing.

6.3 THE PHILOSOPHY OF DSDM ATERN

The philosophy of DSDM Atern is that any project must be:

- Aligned to clearly defined strategic goals
- Focused on early and frequent delivery of real benefits to the business.

To achieve this, key stakeholders must understand the business objectives, be empowered to an appropriate level and collaborate with solution developers and each other to deliver the right solution in the agreed timescales, according to business priorities.

6.4 THE EIGHT PRINCIPLES

DSDM Atern defines eight principles that embody its way of working, are fundamental to the successful application of the approach, and support its philosophy. Compromising any principle constitutes a risk to the on-time and on-budget delivery of the right business-focused solution. The collective value of the principles enables organizations to deliver best-value business solutions promptly, collaboratively, consistently, and of the right quality.

The principles (illustrated in Figure 6.2) are:

- Focus on the business need
- Deliver on time
- Collaborate
- Never compromise quality
- Build incrementally from firm foundations
- Develop iteratively
- Communicate continuously and clearly
- Demonstrate control.

The eight principles are discussed in more detail in the following sections.

- **Principle 1: Focus on the business need** This principle focuses on the true business priorities. MoSCoW prioritization is used to classify requirements as **m**ust have, **s**hould have, **c**ould have and **w**on't have this time. This ensures that the importance of all requirements to the business is understood. The 'must haves' are the minimum usable subset of requirements, which must be delivered for the project to be worthwhile and valuable to the business. DSDM Atern's roles and responsibilities include business roles. Business and end-user representatives work within the project teams, empowered to make day-to-day decisions during the project.

- **Principle 2: Deliver on time** Delivering products on time is often critical for a project. Late delivery can undermine the business case, especially where market opportunities or legal and compliance deadlines are involved. Late delivery also consumes resources that may be needed for other projects. In order to fulfil this principle, DSDM Atern teams must timebox their work and retain a clear focus on business priorities.

Focus on the business need

Build incrementally from firm foundations

Deliver on time

Develop iteratively

Collaborate

Communicate continuously and clearly

Never compromise quality

Demonstrate control

Figure 6.2 The eight DSDM Atern principles

In order to achieve on-time delivery, it actually helps if the teams establish a reputation for timely and predictable deliveries. This way people involved in the timeboxes will expect their involvement to be needed at the planned times and will not be so inclined to double-book their time.

■ **Principle 3: Collaborate**   This principle requires that teams work together towards a common goal, build a one-team approach and actively cooperate and honour their commitments to each other. DSDM Atern teams need consistent involvement of the right people and skills throughout the project. They also need to be empowered. Roles are defined to help with

this. Facilitated workshops enable stakeholders to share knowledge effectively with other members of the team.

■ **Principle 4: Never compromise quality**   In DSDM Atern, the level of quality to be delivered should be agreed at the start. A solution must be fit for purpose – not over-engineered, but of appropriate quality to satisfy the business need. In order to fulfil this principle, DSDM Atern teams need to test throughout the lifecycle and use quality reviews to build in quality from the start. Test-driven techniques may result in a test being written before the deliverable is produced. MoSCoW prioritization and a risk-based approach ensure that testing is appropriate. Documentation of testing should be lean but sufficient.

- **Principle 5: Build incrementally from firm foundations** This principle has two distinct aspects – to build in small, complete chunks (increments) in order to deliver real business benefit early, and sufficiently understand the requirements to mitigate risk. DSDM Atern advocates incremental development, with short timeboxes focused on completed products. This encourages stakeholder confidence, as stakeholders see completed elements of the solution emerging from the very early stages of the project. It also promotes learning and improvement of the solution as increments progress. DSDM Atern teams are urged to do just enough analysis and design upfront to understand the structure and scope of the full solution at a high level. The incremental plan is then focused on early delivery of business benefit within this scope.

- **Principle 6: Develop iteratively** Change is inevitable, so DSDM Atern endeavours to harness its benefits. A defined, iterative approach of investigate, refine and consolidate is embedded within timeboxes to allow the development teams the space to investigate, embrace change, be creative, experiment, learn, and evolve the solution in a controlled way. User involvement allows the team to continually confirm that the correct solution is being built. The evolutionary approach uses modelling and prototyping to make options and solution elements visible.

- **Principle 7: Communicate continuously and clearly** Communication problems are often cited as a key cause of project failure. DSDM Atern teams use rich communication techniques such as modelling and prototyping to make early instances of the solution visible. They also use facilitated workshops to promote involvement and buy-in and to help manage stakeholder expectations throughout the project. Appropriate documentation is needed and this should be kept lean and timely. Informal face-to-face communication should be used where appropriate.

- **Principle 8: Demonstrate control** It is essential to know the status of the project at all times. A DSDM Atern team should be proactive when monitoring and controlling progress. There should be an appropriate level of formality; plans should be visible to necessary stakeholders and progress measured through delivery of completed products. Timeboxing is used to maintain control and achieve visibility of progress. The appropriate roles also evaluate continuing project viability based on the business objectives.

6.5 THE DSDM ATERN LIFECYCLE

DSDM Atern's configurable lifecycle is designed for frequent product delivery, iterative and incremental development, active business involvement, interwoven testing, and early delivery of business benefits.

There are seven phases in the DSDM Atern lifecycle, and there is a product for each one. The seven phases are:

- Pre-project
- Feasibility
- Foundations
- Exploration
- Engineering
- Deployment
- Post-project.

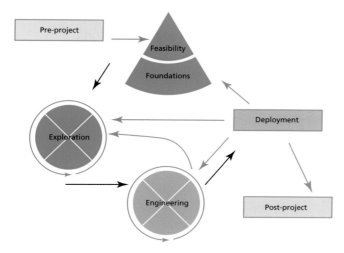

Figure 6.3 The DSDM Atern lifecycle

The arrows in the lifecycle diagram (Figure 6.3) illustrate that the phases of the lifecycle are not purely sequential. For example, pre-project, feasibility and foundations would follow one another, but may then be followed by several repetitions of exploration and engineering before a deployment phase is entered. It is also possible for several deployment phases to occur before closure of the project triggers the post-project phase.

■ **Pre-project**   The pre-project phase establishes the terms of reference for the project. It creates a brief statement justifying the project and prioritizing a feasibility investigation. It must ensure that all key stakeholders can be involved from the start of the feasibility phase.

■ **Feasibility**   The feasibility phase should be short. It seeks to secure project sponsorship, confirm an outline business case for the project and develop an outline plan. Various business and technical solution options will be considered in outline and timescales and costs

will be estimated. The solution scope will be drafted, the problem that the solution must address will be clarified and the chosen options defined.

■ **Foundations**   The foundations phase is aimed at establishing a clear project focus that is robust and flexible. The three essential perspectives of business, solution and management are considered. Clear roles and responsibilities are established, high-level requirements are gathered and their priorities and relevance to the business recorded in a prioritized requirements list (PRL). A more detailed business case is established and project strategy defined.

■ **Exploration and engineering**   The exploration and engineering phases are used to investigate detailed business requirements and evolve them into a viable solution.

The end product of exploration will be refined during the engineering phase to ensure technical acceptance criteria are met and evolved into a working, tested solution. These two phases may occur separately or overlap.

■ **Deployment**   The primary purpose of the deployment phase is to move the solution into live use. It is also a key review point prior to future development work.

The number of passes through the deployment phase will depend on whether it is feasible for the business to accept delivery of the solution incrementally.

■ **Post-project**   The post-project phase takes place after the last planned deployment of the solution. Its purpose is to reflect on the business value actually achieved. This assessment should start as soon as the value can be measured.

6.6 DSDM ATERN TEAMS AND ROLES

DSDM Atern teams have defined roles and responsibilities. The key roles are shown in Figure 6.4.

6.6.1 Project-level roles (managers, coordinators and directors of the project work)

The DSDM project-level roles include a:

- Business sponsor – the senior business person ultimately responsible for the project, who owns the business case and understands the project rationale
- Business visionary – a key business role that communicates the vision and objective for the project to the solution development team on a continual basis throughout the project
- Project manager – responsible for all aspects of the management of the delivery of the solution
- Technical coordinator – the project's technical design authority.

6.6.2 Solution development team roles (shapers and builders of the solution)

Within the solution development team, there will be a:

- Team leader – works with the team to plan and coordinate all aspects of product delivery at a detailed level.
- Business ambassador – a real business user who provides the business perspective for all day-to-day decisions related to the way the solution's fitness for business purpose is defined and implemented. The business ambassador role is also responsible for organizing all user-acceptance testing.
- Business analyst – a person with business analysis skills, responsible for ensuring that the business needs are properly analysed and communicated, so that they can be correctly reflected in the solution.
- Solution developer – a technically skilled person who interprets business requirements and evolves them into a deployable solution.
- Solution tester – a person with testing skills who performs testing in accordance with the technical testing strategy throughout the project. They may support the business ambassador role in enabling user-acceptance testing.

6.6.3 Other roles (other perspectives and specialisms):

Other DSDM Atern roles include:

- Business advisers
- A workshop facilitator
- An Atern coach
- Specialists.

Any one person may have more than one role and some roles may have more than one person assigned to them, depending upon workload and the nature of the project. It is essential that team members accept their responsibilities and work together towards team success, rather than casting blame. DSDM Atern's agile teams are self-directed and self-organizing rather than being tightly managed by the project manager. Each solution development team should be small (with no more than nine members) and consist of appropriate technical and business roles with equal responsibility. A large project will have many solution development teams working in parallel.

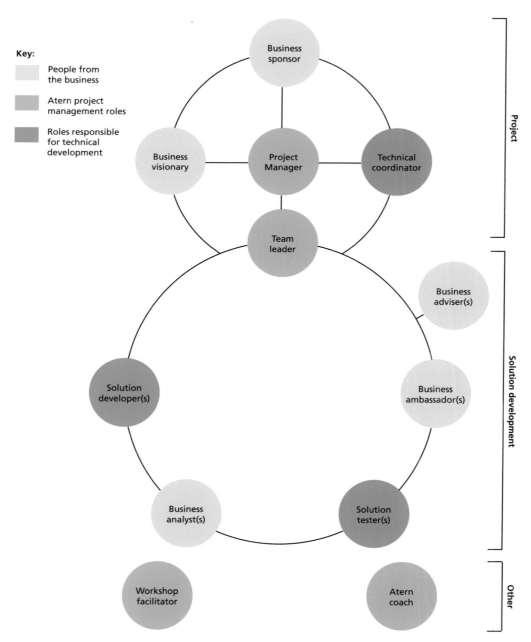

Figure 6.4 Key DSDM Atern roles

6.7 THE BENEFITS OF DSDM ATERN

Some of the main benefits are listed here, although this is not intended to be an exhaustive list:

■ DSDM Atern uses an iterative approach to solution development, so that the final solution can be steered towards the real business needs.

■ The frequent delivery of increments of the solution gives business value early and provides feedback to improve products delivered in future increments. The final solution is more likely to meet users' real business requirements.

■ Users are actively involved throughout the whole development and deployment process, which means that they will be familiar with the solution and feel ownership of it.

■ With real end users working in the DSDM Atern roles throughout the project, the risk of building the wrong solution is greatly reduced.

■ Elements of the evolving solution are prototyped regularly, which provides visibility of the emerging product, a constant check on the solution being evolved and an indication of progress.

■ User representatives have been involved throughout the evolution of the solution and are instrumental in its look, feel and function. These users know the solution well and will be able to act as coaches in the business environment. They can also help to identify other users who will need training.

■ Teamwork between users and developers is established and, as a result, deployment of the solution is more likely to run smoothly given that the team is used to working together.

■ The users know who to talk to if things do not work as they should immediately after deployment.

6.8 SUCCESS FACTORS AND PROJECT RISK

DSDM Atern defines a number of factors instrumental to the success of a project (ISFs):

■ Acceptance of the DSDM Atern philosophy before starting work

■ Appropriate empowerment of the solution development team

■ Commitment of senior business management to provide the necessary user involvement

■ Easy access by solution developers to business roles

■ Solution development team stability

■ Appropriate solution development team skills

■ Small solution development team size

■ A supportive commercial relationship between supplier and customer

■ Appropriate development technology to allow for iterative development, demonstrable work products, and control of the development and release of new versions.

Where these factors cannot be met, it constitutes a risk to the project. A DSDM Atern project approach questionnaire combines these and other criteria into a set of questions, which helps to determine the risks that need to be addressed when applying this approach.

6.9   CONCLUSION

We have considered the overall philosophy of
DSDM Atern, its eight principles, the configurable
lifecycle and team roles. We have looked at the
factors instrumental to success and considered
these in line with risk. We have also seen some of
the key benefits of the approach.

DSDM Atern fixes time and cost, but needs the
set of required features to be flexible in order to
maintain quality. It uses MoSCoW prioritization to
identify the minimum usable subset of features to
meet the business need and controls development
and delivery with clear product-based timeboxes.

The continuous involvement of the right business
representation and a clear focus on business value
predisposes the DSDM Atern project to success.

We have now seen all three best-practice
approaches: PRINCE2, ITIL and DSDM Atern. The
next chapter sees Octagrid embarking on a project
that combines elements of all three.

Set up 7

7 Set up

In this chapter, we cover the setting up of a combined project. Octagrid already has ITIL, PRINCE2 and DSDM Atern in place in different areas of the organization. It is now looking to set up a project using all three together in a combined project.

In this chapter and the three subsequent chapters, you will learn:

- The benefits of merging the three approaches
- Hints and tips on how this can be achieved.

7.1 INTRODUCTION

In this chapter we follow Octagrid as it attempts to deliver a project using ITIL, PRINCE2 and DSDM Atern. But it's not all fiction – the advice and checklists in this chapter have been compiled using experience from real assignments and are transferrable to other projects.

7.2 WHY SHOULD WE USE ITIL, PRINCE2 AND DSDM ATERN TOGETHER?

We are eavesdropping on a management meeting at Octagrid. The chief executive officer (CEO) is chairing, the head of new development projects is looking worried and the marketing director is muttering that this strategy should be abandoned. The head of consultancy is describing the vision, with some passion, arguing: 'A document management system for our consultants across the world will reduce the load on the service desk and could dramatically reduce the number of operatives we need.'

'But we have to do it right,' adds the head of new development projects. 'We'll need an enormous amount of storage capacity for all the documents. Capacity management needs to know about this, and we'll also have to consider information security and availability – in fact, all of the ITIL service management areas. We also need to consider what the consultants want. Still, at least this won't be a time-critical project ...'

'Excuse me, but it is time-critical,' warns the CEO. 'I don't want this project to run on forever. I want to know how much it will cost and I want a return on the investment quickly. What's more, if this project is running aground, I want to know immediately so that we can prevent any more money being wasted. You remember that first web project ...' The CEO takes a sip of coffee and lets the memory of the previous embarrassing project hang in the air for a moment.

The issues highlight why combining ITIL, PRINCE2 and DSDM Atern can be so successful. Merging the three approaches ensures:

- The involvement of the right representatives/ stakeholders throughout (see Figure 7.1, which shows what needs to be considered and who needs to be involved in a change project)
- Tight control over time, cost, functionality and quality
- Provision of a safe, secure and maintainable system.

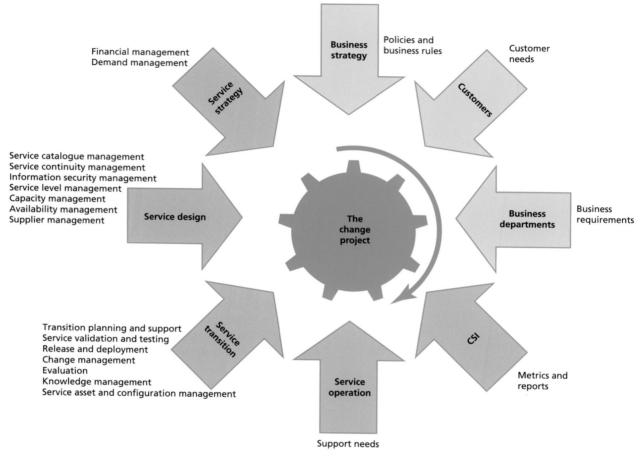

Figure 7.1 Pressures on the change project

7.3 USING ITIL, PRINCE2 AND DSDM ATERN TOGETHER

7.3.1 What problems are we trying to solve?

In previous chapters we looked at some of the problems that can arise when using ITIL, PRINCE2 and DSDM Atern separately. A recurring problem was that service management staff do not always understand the project world, and change project workers do not understand service management responsibilities and structures. In addition, PRINCE2 does not give guidance on people management and team working, whilst DSDM Atern is not always considered to have sufficiently strong governance. The problems identified in Chapters 1, 3 and 5 have been analysed and consolidated in Table 7.1. For each problem area, Octagrid has identified actions that it will take in order to mitigate these problems.

Table 7.1 Addressing the problems of the three approaches

Problem area	Action
Process and standards	
Lack of clarity of the service management interface with the change project process	Create a combined service-and-project lifecycle linking ITIL, PRINCE2 and DSDM (Chapter 11 proposes a roadmap for this)
	Create clear guidance for areas of overlap
Lack of knowledge and understanding between the ITIL world and the project world	Train service management and change-project staff in ITIL, PRINCE2 and DSDM Atern
	Establish mixed-skill teams
	Establish a common glossary of terms to use (see Glossaries)
No coordination of the promised go-live date with service management	Create a project checklist for sign-off and release, with named representatives from the project, service management and the business (see Table 7.4). Put the ITIL project checklist in place at the beginning of the project
	Ensure the project is entered into the ITIL forward schedule of change
Service asset and configuration management standards not followed in projects	Create project initiation documentation from PRINCE2, with quality management strategy, configuration management strategy and communication plan
The conventions used by new applications are not consistent with other applications in the service	Ensure common style guides are produced
Stakeholders and roles	
The right stakeholders are not always involved or, if they are, not early enough in the projects	Identify a standard list of project stakeholders including service management
(No service management roles were invited to be involved)	Identify roles and responsibilities for the project
Requirements	
Requirements for availability, fall-back and recovery, maintainability, capacity, security, and ITSCM have not been taken into account	Identify non-functional requirements by involving ITIL roles in addition to business representatives
Culture	
Lack of cultural alignment between the waterfall, structured world of ITIL and PRINCE2 and the collaborative, facilitative world of DSDM Atern	Encourage respect for the skills of each other's roles and collaborative team management in both projects and service management
Techniques	
Leadership and people management, team working and collaboration are needed	DSDM Atern offers the most support in this area

Table 7.1 Addressing the problems of the three approaches *continued*

Projects run over time and budget	Use PRINCE2 tolerances
	Use PRINCE2 work packages
	Use DSDM Atern timeboxing for low-level control
	Use MoSCoW prioritization
Poor communication	Keep plans visible to all, on walls and in collaboration tools
	Keep teams small and multi-skilled
	Use facilitated workshops and daily stand-ups
Poor estimating	Use DSDM Atern estimating guidance
	Use timeboxing for early warning of overruns
	Use PRINCE2 management stages

7.3.2 Which parts of each method should we use?

Chapter 11 gives a complete mapping between the approaches, based on the key features that each approach can bring to a project. The Venn diagram in Figure 7.2 is a simple schematic of this mapping. Some features overlap two or more approaches, indicating that they are mentioned in more than one approach. When a feature overlaps two or more of the approaches, it is more developed in the one approach into which it overlaps. For example, MoSCoW prioritization is now mentioned in all three approaches, but it is most developed within DSDM Atern; facilitated workshops are explained within ITIL, but full guidance is given in DSDM Atern.

7.4 SETTING UP THE COMBINED PROJECT

Octagrid's project is for the provision of a document management system to support its worldwide network of associate consultants, supported by the head office service desk. A major part of the project is the acquisition and customization of a standard applications software package from a third-party supplier.

The project is called the COMMANDO (**c**onsultancy **m**anaged **m**edia **and d**ocument **o**rganizing) system.

7.4.1 The objectives

7.4.1.1 *Business reason for the project*

Associate consultants across the world need access to centrally held information about customer accounts, orders and previous projects. They also need access to the latest marketing information about the tools that Octagrid sells. Remote access to the computers at head office from hotels, offices and airports abroad has not only proved slow and time-consuming, but it is also considered a security risk. Consultants often telephone the service desk requesting the information they need. This places a heavy load on the service desk.

It is estimated that if a document management system could be installed, to which all consultants had access, the reduction in workload on head office staff would be equivalent to four full-time staff – a significant saving to be offset against the cost of the document management system.

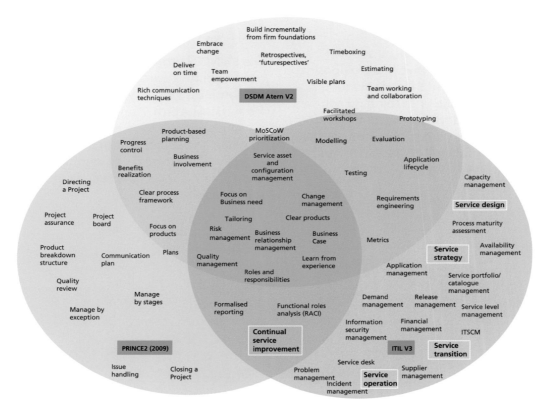

Figure 7.2 Venn diagram showing the overlapping of PRINCE2, DSDM Atern and ITIL features

7.4.1.2 Project objective

The objective of the project is to provide the associate consultants, wherever they are in the world, with a cost-effective and timely way of seeing **all** company documents related to a customer or a tool.

This will directly lead to cost savings, the provision of a better service to the customer and increased tool sales, which will enhance the reputation and profitability of Octagrid.

Octagrid will use PRINCE2 as the overarching governance framework for the project and integrate DSDM Atern and ITIL into this. The CEO has issued the project mandate, making the head of consultancy the executive, and the project is now officially in the Starting up a Project process.

7.4.2 The birth of the project

The project mandate has been issued and the new project is authorized to start. PRINCE2 will have overall control of the project, but DSDM Atern and ITIL will be woven into the project throughout its life. For example, service design will need to assess the proposed change in line with business and IT service strategy; capacity and availability management will need to ensure that the non-functional requirements can be met without compromising other existing services; supplier management will need to be involved in choosing the supplier of the document management software and setting up the underpinning contract and, when the supplier developers join the team of internal developers and users to customize the package, they will be following the DSDM Atern principles and practices.

7.4.3 Setting up the project management team

The PRINCE2 project management team roles and responsibilities are adopted, with the addition of a business visionary and technical coordinator from DSDM Atern. Appropriate ITIL representation is included in the form of a senior user, senior supplier, and user and supplier focus groups. Figure 7.3 illustrates the combined project roles and Table 7.2 shows the specific Octagrid resources taking on these roles.

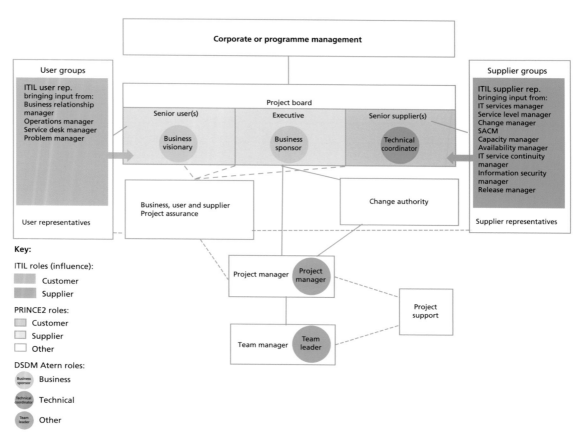

Figure 7.3 Combined PRINCE2, DSDM Atern and ITIL project roles

Table 7.2 Octagrid resources

Role	Octagrid person	Reason for choice
Executive	Head of consultancy	Business role, budgetary control
Senior User 1	Head of consultancy	Representing consultants who are key users of this service
Senior User 2	ITIL operations manager	Representing service desk operatives, who are key users (and super users) of this service
Business visionary	Head of consultancy	The business person with the passion and vision for this change, a sufficient overview of the business to prioritize, and the seniority to make the change happen
Technical coordinator	Service design manager/technical architect	The person with the technical vision for this change, sufficient overview of the service portfolio to prioritize and the seniority to make decisions regarding application and infrastructure
Senior Supplier 1	Head of IT new developments department	Supplier of software (Octagrid considered having the document management supplier representative in this role but the executive decided not, as the project board is a decision-making body. The supplier's input will be managed by the head of IT new developments department)
Senior Supplier 2	ITIL service manager	Supplier of support and infrastructure
User group	Selected focus group of consultants from various areas, including the service desk	
Supplier group	Selected focus group of ITIL managers, plus the third-party supplier of the document management software	
Project assurance	Performed by project board members	
Change authority	Performed by project board members	
Project manager	The project manager from the DSDM Atern implementation in Chapter 5	Has DSDM Atern experience, and recently PRINCE2 and ITIL trained

The project manager, visionary, technical coordinator and executive, with input from the senior suppliers and senior users, set out a project brief (with an outline business case) and initiation stage plan. In line with the DSDM Atern philosophy, the project brief is kept short and 'just sufficient'. The project approach within the project brief is checked by service design for alignment with service strategy. The ITIL change manager notes that the change project is authorized and tentative dates and details are entered into the forward schedule of change (FSC) and the service pipeline.

A project brief and initiation stage plan are submitted for project board authorization, which is given.

7.4.3.1 Special features

At the end of Starting up a Project, the combined project has the following special features:

- The project brief is concise (adhering to the DSDM Atern philosophy of 'do enough and no more')
- A prototype was used to demonstrate the proposed product to the project board (prototyping – DSDM Atern)
- ITIL representation and a DSDM Atern (visionary) role are included in the project board
- The DSDM Atern project approach questionnaire has been used to establish an agile approach to the project.

7.4.4 Initiating a Project

This is where, in DSDM Atern terms, the firm foundations for the project (business, management and solution) are established.

PRINCE2's influence is to set up strategies for:

- Risk management
- Quality management
- Configuration management
- Communication management, controls and reporting.

The outcome of this process is the project initiation documentation (PID) and a first stage plan.

DSDM Atern's influence is to:

- Ensure that the first stage plan and the project plan are clearly timeboxed and incremental deliveries have been considered and planned, as appropriate
- Plan daily stand-ups as a means of checkpoint reporting between the solution development team and the project manager

- Set up facilitated workshops for project kick-off, visioning, risk and stakeholder analysis
- Bring solution development team members on board to collaboratively estimate and plan the first stage
- MoSCoW prioritize the product breakdown structure and the initial high-level prioritized requirements list (PRL).

ITIL's influence is to:

- Ensure project strategies align with service management standards
- Ensure that the project approach is in line with service strategy
- Ensure that the design of the service is in line with service design strategy
- Identify key non-functional requirements and constraints – ensure requirements related to other ITIL disciplines are captured, e.g. requirements related to capacity, availability, security, continuity and service level agreements already in place
- Ensure that incremental release dates are feasible and are recorded in the FSC
- Ensure service design, service transition and service operation activities are included in the plans and estimates
- Ensure that the risks and impacts of service transition and early life support are included in the business case.

7.4.4.1 Solution development team roles

The DSDM Atern roles and responsibilities are the best basis for the solution development team, of which there may be more than one (see Figure 7.4).

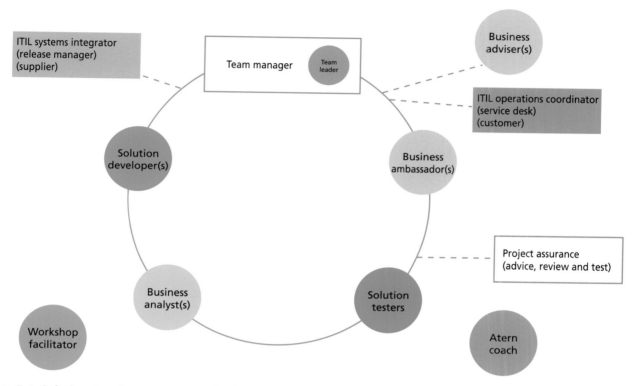

Figure 7.4 Solution development team roles in a combined project

ITIL roles are also represented in the solution development team – service management is **not** running a separate design project and a separate release project. Service design and service transition activities are performed iteratively and from **within** the change project. In Table 7.3 the roles marked with an asterisk (*) are proposed new roles, required to integrate ITIL, DSDM Atern and PRINCE2.

The fact that service transition testing skill is used in the solution development team in this combined project significantly changes the profile of work for this role – from one that works in a block after the change project has delivered, to being continually needed throughout the project.

Each solution development team is a small mixed-skill team of seven, plus or minus two, people with the right combination of user and supplier skills to achieve the objectives of the project (see Figure 7.5). The suggested number of people in the team (seven plus or minus two) is known as Miller's limit, and based on the work of psychologist George Miller.

Table 7.3 Solution development team roles in the COMMANDO project

Role	Octagrid person	Reason for choice
Team manager	As chosen by the agile team	
Business analyst	Service designer	The skill could come from the IT new developments department or service design. Note: this is not technical design, which is provided by the technical coordinator role and solution developers
Business ambassador(s)	Associate consultant (as needed from each separate user area)	Service desk operatives are also business-user roles, but are included as ITIL operations coordinators
Business advisers	Someone from the business side, as needed for review and testing	This is user-validation testing, not technical verification
Solution tester	Service transition tester	Service transition has the technical testing skills and resources
Solution developer(s)	Developers	Both third-party developers and internal developers are team members. Some solution developer roles may be service management hardware and network-skilled technical staff
ITIL operations coordinator (*)	Service desk operative (user representative)	This role ensures that requirements for service support are properly addressed
ITIL systems integrator (*)	Release manager (supplier representative)	This role coordinates the transition planning and release planning activities and also brings requirements into the team from the other ITIL disciplines at a detailed level, since it would be impractical to involve every ITIL role directly. The supplier group will support this role

A larger project will have several solution development teams, with the technical coordinator ensuring integrity of product elements produced by each team. The technical coordinator is also, typically, the inter-team role with responsibility for configuration management.

7.4.4.2 Special features

At the end of Initiating a Project, the combined project has the following special features:

- The PID is slimmer than usual (led by the lean documentation philosophy of DSDM Atern)
- A demonstration prototype of the proposed product has been presented to the project board (DSDM Atern)

- A timeboxed, incremental, feature-based project plan is in place (PRINCE2 plus DSDM Atern)
- A timeboxed, incremental feature-based stage plan is in place, with early and incremental complete deliverables (PRINCE2 plus DSDM Atern)
- ITIL representation and products are visibly included (ITIL)
- Early life support activities are integrated with deliveries throughout the project (ITIL).

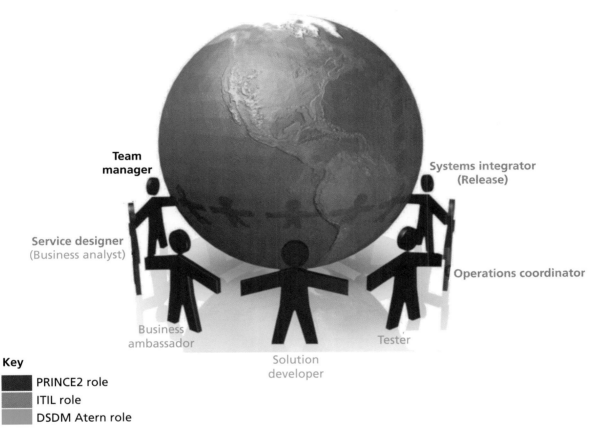

Figure 7.5 The solution development team

The project board approves the plans and empowers the teams to use the flexibility of the 'should have' and 'could have' requirements, as needed. The project board authorizes the project (and in Chapter 8 we shall see how the project actually runs).

7.5 CHECKLISTS FOR STARTING UP AND INITIATING THE COMBINED PROJECT

The following hints, tips and checklists are intended to be generic to all combined projects.

7.5.1 Checklists for assisting a good project start-up and initiation

Good existing resources for the project manager are:

■ The PRINCE2 health check: Appendix E of *Managing Successful Projects with PRINCE2™*

■ The DSDM Atern project approach questionnaire: *DSDM Atern The Handbook*.

There is no readily available ITIL checklist for this purpose, and so one is compiled in Table 7.4. This will also form the basis of a go-live checklist, for handover to ITIL service operations.

Table 7.4 ITIL project checklist

	Question	ITIL role involved	Project role involved
1	Has the change (project mandate) been authorized?	Change manager	Executive Project manager
2	Have service level requirements been agreed?	Business relationship manager	Project manager
3	Has the project's intended delivery date (or dates) been agreed and entered into the FSC?	Change manager	Project manager
4	Has the budget been approved for project costs?	Financial manager	Executive Project manager
5	Have third-party suppliers been identified and vetted, and underpinning contracts or framework agreements established?	Supplier manager	Project manager
6	Has organizational project risk been analysed, and are there plans in place to manage it?	Risk management*	Project manager
7	Have training requirements been planned for all support areas?	Service desk, incident management	Project manager
8	Have potential capacity impacts been analysed over the short, medium and long term?	Capacity manager	Project manager
9	Have service reporting needs been agreed?	CSI service reporting	Project manager
10	Have IT service continuity and availability requirements been planned for?	ITSCM and availability management	Project manager
11	Have security requirements been planned for?	Information security management	Project manager

*Note: Risk management is not a separate function in ITIL, but mentioned throughout the disciplines. Organizational risk is typically a business-strategic function.

7.5.2 Hints and tips

The following hints and tips for setting up a combined project may be useful for those looking to adopt a similar three-approach project:

- Roles:
  - Think about who you really need in the project before allocating roles
  - Do not leave out any roles and do not create any roles without defining their responsibilities
  - Ensure people have understood their responsibilities and accepted them
  - Do a stakeholder analysis early on in the project, so that those who need to be involved have been identified when roles are allocated, and review it during the project
  - One person can hold more than one role and, for some roles, one role could be held by more than one person
  - Ensure that each member of the team realizes their time commitment to this type of project and has been involved in estimating and planning.

- Planning:
  - Devise a plan based on completing business-valuable features, which are delivered incrementally (ensuring business value is delivered early)
  - Plan features and complete products, not tasks.
- Prototyping (from DSDM Atern) will help to establish a clear, shared vision and early testing.
- Establish communications early. Take ownership of a project room, which can then be used as a designated place for workshops and collaborative working. Co-locate the team, where possible, for the duration of the project. Where this is not possible (and it often is not!) the team still needs a location (even a virtual one) where plans can be made visible and facilitated workshops can be held, sometimes at short notice. Teleconferencing facilities and intranet collaboration tools may be part of this.
- Run facilitated workshops to establish everyone's involvement from the outset.
- Brief the whole project team on the differences of this type of combined project (compared to one using, for example, PRINCE2 alone) at the beginning of the project.
- Train the teams, the project board and the users, and inform and educate other stakeholders on the differences of this approach.
- Set up daily stand-ups and retrospectives (review workshops). Allow time for these in the plans.
- Rely on PRINCE2 for the management products, but take an agile DSDM Atern attitude to them ('enough and no more') and look to the ITIL service design package and service transition package for key elements to include.

7.6   CONCLUSION

In this chapter we have kicked-off the project, using PRINCE2, ITIL and DSDM Atern. We have seen where the strengths of each approach lie and have gathered some hints and tips for capitalizing on the best aspects of each. In Chapter 8 we shall see how the combined project runs.

Run! 8

8 Run!

This chapter covers:

- How the combined project runs
- What the plans look like
- How timeboxing works with work packages
- Where the ITIL touch points are.

In this chapter you will learn:

- How ITIL, PRINCE2 and DSDM Atern work together whilst the project is running
- Hints and tips from experience.

8.1 INTRODUCTION

In this chapter we will look at how Octagrid's COMMANDO project runs (the 'controlled progress' elements of the combined project). We will also consider some of the factors affecting the incremental delivery of a product when using DSDM Atern, PRINCE2 and ITIL. The timeboxed plan for the project (now scheduled for six months) is shown in Figure 8.1.

This is where the real work of the project is done – producing new products and services for measurable business benefit. For DSDM Atern, this means moving from foundations into exploration, engineering and deployment; for ITIL, it means that the disciplines of service design and service transition will be used in an incremental and iterative way; and for PRINCE2 it means that Controlling a Stage, Managing Product Delivery and the decision points associated with Managing a Stage Boundary have to be carried out, with governance elements of Directing a Project involved both at stage boundaries and during stages.

8.1.1 Managing the culture

There are significant cultural differences to be managed in this project. The agile project espouses iterative development and incremental delivery of products to give early business value. Although ITIL v3 mentions iterative working, the ITIL guidance strongly implies a waterfall approach to service design and service delivery (see Figure 8.2). Service design produces a service design package (SDP) with requirements specified in considerable detail, if the suggested SDP template from the ITIL *Service Design* publication (TSO, 2007) is used. The PRINCE2 process framework allows for an iterative approach, but the waterfall approach has been traditionally used there too.

In this combined project, service delivery will receive incremental deliveries of part of the final solution and can work on these deliveries of functionality early, while the project is still in progress. In a pure waterfall environment, service delivery would not become involved until the whole product was given to it to transition into 'live'.

The project manager will have to promote a different culture and motivate the teams in their new agile and iterative way of working.

Because this is an agile project, there should be an empowered solution development team and collaborative leadership from the project manager. The co-location of the solution development team,

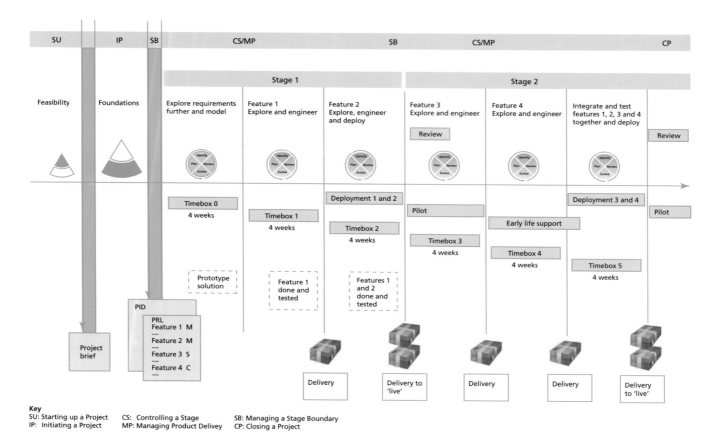

Figure 8.1 The timeboxed plan for the project

where possible, can help the different disciplines understand and respect each other's opinions. In addition, training team members from each discipline, to some extent, in the other methods will aid team understanding. The use of facilitated workshops will also help to generate buy-in and collaboration.

The project management role is now quite different from the traditional management style of controlling teams and tasking individuals. Agile project teams operate within a culture of self-direction and self-organization – with a much greater emphasis on team-based empowerment than would have traditionally been the case. The individual risk of this to the project manager is the feeling of relinquishing control. However, this is offset by the liberation of team ingenuity and team ownership of deadlines.

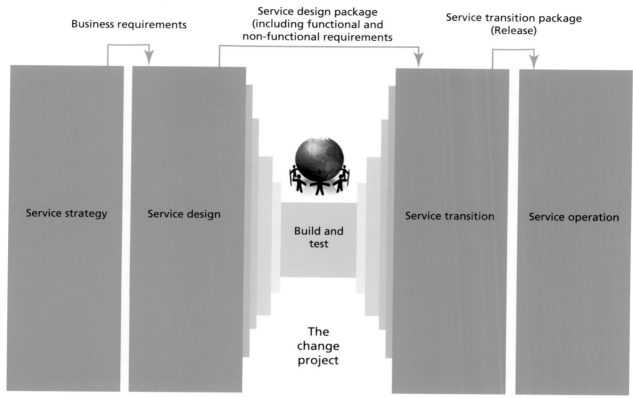

Figure 8.2 ITIL and the change project in a waterfall relationship

8.2 CONTROLLING A STAGE AND MANAGING PRODUCT DELIVERY

8.2.1 The plan for delivery

PRINCE2, ITIL and DSDM Atern have an ongoing influence on the change project. The alignment of their lifecycles is illustrated in Figure 8.3 and mapped in Chapter 11.

8.2.2 Options for delivery

The pattern of delivery for Octagrid's COMMANDO project was set in the stage plan by the project manager and solution development team in a facilitated workshop during the Initiating a Project process. This enabled each team member to influence the estimates and only agree to what they believed they could achieve. The concept of team commitment is fundamental here. Everyone in the team is relying on other team members to do what is expected of them.

Various options for configuring the DSDM Atern lifecycle were available to the team. They are illustrated in Figure 8.4 and include:

■ Deliver something into 'live' at the end of every timebox. This would have placed a large

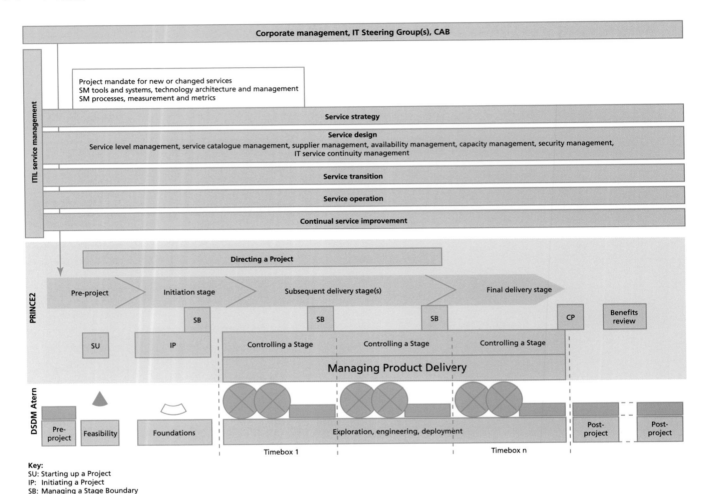

Key:
SU: Starting up a Project
IP: Initiating a Project
SB: Managing a Stage Boundary
CP: Closing a Project

Figure 8.3 The involvements of PRINCE2, DSDM Atern and ITIL in the change project

overhead – associated with delivery, pilot and early life support – on continued development.

■ Just one delivery at the end of the project. The project would not benefit from the delivery of early business value, and it would introduce risk by not having a clear early check on progress, which would be proven by the delivery of an element of working product early in the project.

■ Do all of the exploration (analysis and design) before the engineering (build and test). However, the benefit of delivering completed, explored and engineered chunks is that something complete can be delivered earlier on in the project, and lessons learned from these can be used to improve later ones.

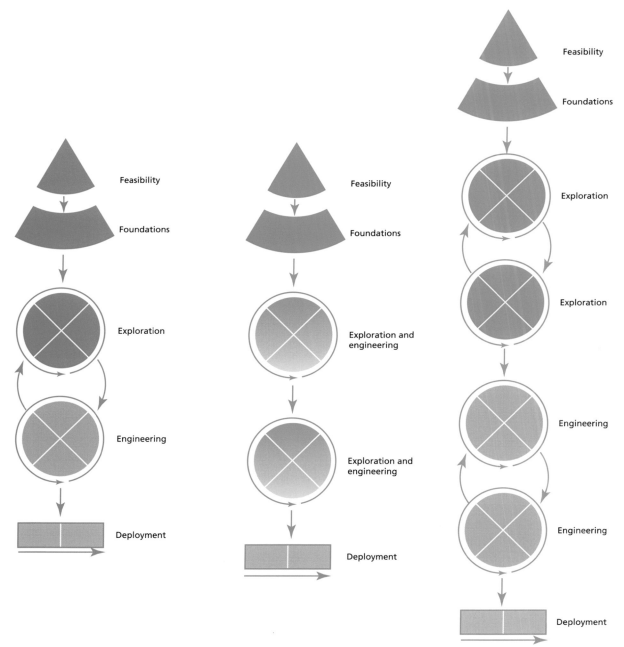

Figure 8.4 Options for configuring the DSDM Atern lifecycle

The CEO wants to have in place an early failure warning, which is why an incremental delivery plan (timeboxed plan) has been chosen (see Figure 8.1).

With project board input, the team has decided on two management stages within the six-month timeframe, with three one-month timeboxes per stage and delivery at the end stage (as illustrated in the project plan in Figure 8.1). Although it is usual to plan one stage at a time, the shortness of the stages has allowed for two planned stages to be shown here.

A high-level, prioritized set of requirements, available at the end of Initiating a Project, is sufficient for agreement, planning and prioritization. The prioritized requirements list (PRL) would typically be quality reviewed and signed off by key stakeholders to form a baseline for the scope of the project. The PRL is supported by the project initiation documentation (PID), which includes a prioritized product breakdown structure. More detailed requirements are elicited, timebox by timebox, as the project progresses and completed, tested features emerge from each timebox. These may be planned for release into 'live' at this point.

It is usually beneficial to have a 'Timebox 0' after initiation in order to establish an overview of the whole project and ensure standards are known and understood, environments are set up, and communication mechanisms are in place. This timebox is not likely to produce a tested, feature-based deliverable, but should have a clear outcome needed for the project.

ITIL's service design and service transition activities will occur at a high level during Starting up a Project and Initiating a Project and then repeatedly throughout the timeline of the project. ITIL representatives will work within the project team throughout the project. This has a great impact on the working profile of ITIL staff, particularly those from release management and service transition (testing).

8.2.3 Work packages

Work packages operate well with timeboxes. Typically, the relationship would be one work package per timebox, per team – although it would be possible to plan more than one work package per timebox per team, if this made the deliverables clearer. Work packages should represent complete features with clear business value. Work package tolerances can be used, but time tolerance is not needed as the scope is adjustable by the empowered timebox team, based on pre-agreed MoSCoW prioritization. The team has the power to de-scope 'could have' and 'should have' requirements, but changes to 'must haves' would involve PRINCE2 escalation procedures.

8.2.4 Working within a timebox

The work within a development timebox (see Figure 8.5) typically follows the pattern of investigation, refinement and consolidation, and what emerges is a complete and tested piece of working product. There is always a kick-off for the team (often a workshop) to establish agreement on the product of the timebox and to clarify its acceptance criteria. The team works through the timebox, with daily stand-ups, to give the team, and the project manager in particular, visibility of progress. Progress can be monitored by these daily stand-ups which replace written checkpoint reports, thereby covering the PRINCE2 activity of

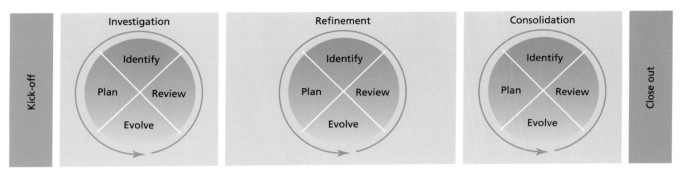

Figure 8.5 The DSDM Atern development timebox

'review work package status'. The timebox ends with a close-out (again, probably a workshop) to ensure that all work is complete, to review the achievements of the timebox and to discuss lessons learned and improvements that could be made to the process (possibly using a retrospective workshop).

8.2.5 Testing the timebox product

Within an agile project, testing takes place throughout a timebox – testing as much as possible, as soon as possible. This means that all levels of testing for a particular feature need to be carried out within the timebox, and documented in a lean but sufficient way. Service transition staff will have the greatest testing expertise in an organization, as they are responsible for ensuring that any change is stable and integrates into the IT infrastructure without causing disruption to existing services (we will look at this integration role in more depth in Chapter 9). However, as the solution testers in the solution development team, the service transition staff must now use their testing skills, offering a level of independence and supporting the other team roles.

The solution tester is not the only role that is responsible for testing. Within an agile team,

everyone is responsible for testing – this is not just a generic statement like 'everyone is responsible for quality'; it is a specific requirement. Everyone creates and ensures the running of their own tests – the business analyst has not fully expressed a requirement unless it contains its own acceptance criteria; the business ambassador brings requirements, scenarios and detailed acceptance criteria to the team and is responsible for carrying out user acceptance testing against these criteria (supported by a working group of business advisers); the solution developer unit-tests their own work and, in some development environments, may even write the tests first, before any code is written (an agile practice known as test-first or test-driven development).

When a timebox is complete, the product under construction is finished, fully tested in its own right and, if this is an engineering-phase timebox, 'production ready'.

8.2.6 Handling issues

Of course, things don't always go according to plan. When issues do occur, the project manager will make recourse to PRINCE2 for change control and issue handling. However, in an agile project certain tolerance-threatening situations can be averted without the need for this – via the solution development team's empowerment to de-scope 'could have' and 'should have' requirements. This is conducted by working collaboratively with the business ambassadors and, in fact, the whole team. It is a powerful way to get back on track. Timeboxes make it visible daily whether this empowerment needs to be invoked.

8.3 MANAGING STAGE BOUNDARIES

Stage boundaries for the COMMANDO project have been planned after each major release. It may be necessary to plan some review time for the timebox teams around this point in order to allow the project board a small amount of decision-making time. However, the project board should understand that the effect of unexpected delay in a timeboxed project is the potential loss of functionality, rather than the moving of timebox deadlines.

8.4 HINTS AND TIPS

Here are a few of the lessons drawn from the COMMANDO project:

■ Ensure that human resources, especially the business ambassadors, are given authorized time that they can dedicate to the project. If they are still 100% involved in their 'day job' they will have insufficient time to dedicate to the project.

■ It is better, although not essential, to have dedicated development resources on an incremental, timeboxed project because of the immovability of timebox deadlines. If resources must be shared between projects, the allocation of dedicated days per week to the project can work well.

■ To ensure focus and control, it is essential that plans are visible to the whole team – this includes governance roles, solution development team members, and user and supplier groups. This is where the availability of a project room (often called a war room) is useful, because plans and developing project artefacts can be kept, visibly, in one location. If co-location of the team is not an option, virtual intranet and internet project environments can work well, but should be supplemented wherever possible by face-to-face communication.

■ Clarity of the prioritized list of requirements and the ongoing changes to what will be delivered is essential.

The iterative project represents a stark change of working pattern from traditional projects. The continued involvement of service design and service transition activities needs careful planning in the early stages. Service design has input at initiation (Initiating a Project), relating the requirements to service strategy and service design. The business analyst role is the guardian of the requirements throughout the project.

8.5 CONCLUSION

The timeboxed plan links PRINCE2 and DSDM Atern lifecycle frameworks, and involves business ambassadors and ITIL representatives.

The biggest challenges here are to the normal working structures of service design, service transition and service operation. Service design is traditionally only peripherally involved in a change project (or, in some cases, not involved at all). In this publication we recommend the ongoing involvement of service design to ensure the alignment of change projects to service strategy and service design.

Service transition is traditionally only invoked at the end of a change project, when it takes over responsibility for testing and deployment, and its involvement continues after the change project has closed. Here, we are recommending the overlapping of service transition with the change project, and the inclusion of personnel from service transition in the change project's solution development teams.

Service operation is also much more involved in the change project here than it would have been traditionally. Service operation is both a customer of the project's products and a supplier of the service to other customers. It also needs to be represented in the solution development team.

We shall look further at the closure of a project and the formal handover to service operation in the next chapter.

9

Deliver!

9 Deliver!

In this chapter we cover:

■ Handover into live. Release management, availability management, capacity management and configuration management all loom large.

In this chapter, you will learn:

■ How ITIL, PRINCE2 and DSDM Atern work together for delivery of the project products
■ Hints and tips from experience.

9.1 INTRODUCTION

The Octagrid COMMANDO project, combining PRINCE2, DSDM Atern and ITIL, is getting ready to deliver its first increment into the live environment. We are in the PRINCE2 process of Controlling a Stage, and DSDM Atern and ITIL service transition have an important role to play.

The ITIL discipline of service transition states: 'Effective service transition can significantly improve a service provider's ability to handle high volumes of change and releases' (*Service Transition* TSO, 2007). This sounds ideally suited to Octagrid's agile project, with its incremental deliveries. In this chapter, we shall see how DSDM Atern and ITIL, within a PRINCE2 framework, can be blended to achieve successful incremental deliveries.

9.2 SERVICE TRANSITION AND DEPLOYMENT

Focusing on Octagrid's COMMANDO project, we are following the plan presented in Chapter 8 (Figure 9.1 shows an extract from this plan).

Feature 1 has been completed on time, is fully unit tested and has been signed off, but it has not yet been delivered into the live environment. The document management package has been configured and functionality is there for a basic set of customer documents to be accessed remotely; the procedures for using the document management package have been customized for Octagrid. A few 'could have' aspects of the feature were de-scoped, by agreement, and are visible on a 'won't have' list in the project room, for clarity.

From a PRINCE2 perspective, stage one of the project is still in progress and within tolerances. Daily stand-ups have kept the project manager informed of progress and the project manager has been submitting weekly highlight reports to the project board.

The Octagrid team is just about to start Timebox 2. Timebox 2 is concerned, firstly, with building Feature 2, and then with the transition and deployment of Features 1 and 2.

9.3 TESTING AND COMPLETION OF FEATURE 1

When a timebox is complete, the product under construction is finished, fully tested in its own right and, for an engineering-phase timebox 'production ready'. Feature 1 is in this completed state. However, it still needs to be tested for integration with other features as they arrive.

The test entry and exit criteria were developed during the exploration and engineering phases

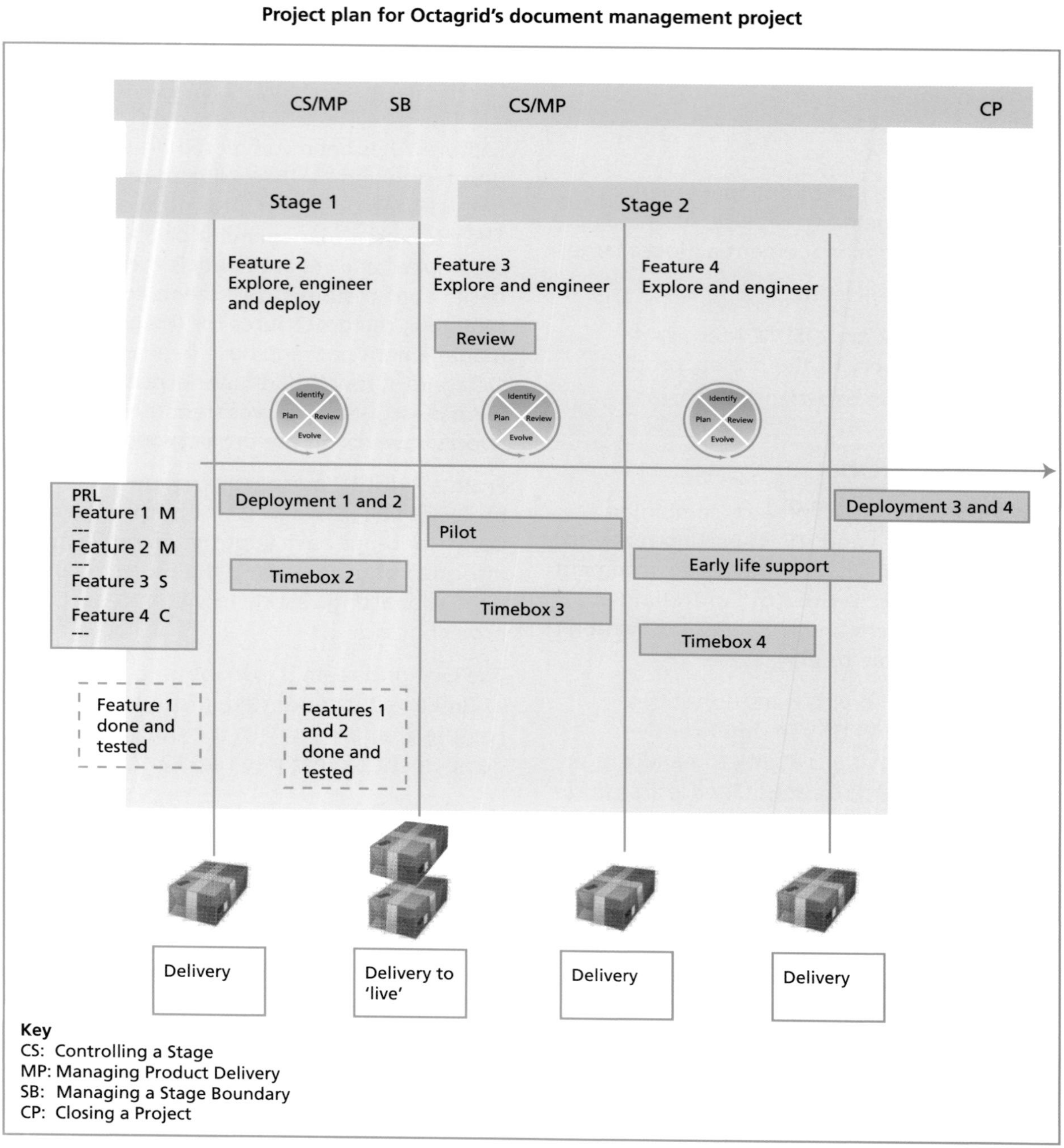

Project plan for Octagrid's document management project

Figure 9.1 An extract from the plan for the COMMANDO project

within Timebox 1, with support from the service design-skilled business analyst role and the service transition-skilled solution tester in the solution development team. The test and entry criteria cover:

- Service design (functional, management and operational)
- Technology design
- Process design
- Measurement design
- Documentation
- Skills and knowledge
- User acceptance.

As much of the testing as possible has been done during Timebox 1 and documented to prevent the unnecessary duplication of testing during deployment and service transition. However, some testing always remains – to integration test, performance test and benchmark the product before release.

In ITIL v3, the service V-model is used to represent the five levels of configuration and testing that are recommended. The five levels are:

- **Level one: customer and business needs** – testing that the service is fit for purpose and fit for use by the business users and customers
- **Level two: service requirements** – testing that service acceptance criteria are met
- **Level three: service solution** – testing operational readiness of the service
- **Level four: service release** – testing that the release can be installed, built and tested in the target environment without disruption to other services, and ensuring that the back-out plans work in case of failure

- **Level five: components and assemblies** – testing that the assembled service matches its SLAs.

Testing, as described by ITIL, is a separate process from the build process, because of the thoroughness of testing required for a successful deployment of a new or changed service into the live production environment. However, many elements of testing are best done early, to prevent fundamental flaws from persisting until it is too late to address them. If we test as much as we can as soon as we can, then the only testing that is left to the end is that which needs to be at the end! Therefore, testing should be integrated throughout – but understand the complexity and necessity for all levels of testing before making a safe deployment to live.

All of these levels of testing need to be completed during Timebox 2 (in addition to building Feature 2 and testing it) if Features 1 and 2 are to be released into the live environment, as planned, at the end of Timebox 2. In addition, before any deployment into the live environment, ITIL also advises that fully tested back-out plans are in place, should there be an unforeseen problem. There are also other aspects of deployment to be considered – such as user training, physical readiness of the office environment, data loading and many other implementation and deployment tasks. Has Octagrid set itself an impossible timebox in Timebox 2? It probably has! However, there should be flexibility in the timebox deliverables, because all timeboxes should contain some requirements with priorities of 'should have' and 'could have', in addition to the 'must have' requirements. It will, therefore, be possible to negotiate the de-scoping of some of these less important requirements in order to deliver the essentials on time, and without compromising quality.

9.4 TIMEBOX 2: A COMPLEX TIMEBOX

9.4.1 DSDM Atern exploration and engineering

Feature 2 has to be built, configured and tested. The supplier solution developers must work with the in-house solution developers, the business ambassadors, the solution tester and the operations coordinator, transferring skills and ensuring that correct knowledge of the package is available. The business analyst(s) representing the business strategy and service design is guardian of the requirements and the integrity of the solution, with input from the business visionary and technical coordinator. Once Feature 2 has been built, Features 1 and 2 then have to be tested together.

9.4.2 ITIL Service transition and DSDM Atern deployment phase

Features 1 and 2 need to be system tested, integration tested and user-acceptance tested. The solution development team is responsible for this, with the ITIL systems integrator and solution tester roles bringing the right ITIL and DSDM Atern testing skills. In this way the testing can be sufficiently independent and thorough, but avoid unnecessary duplication. Both DSDM Atern and ITIL give extensive advice on testing – DSDM Atern's perspective is for the agile project.

The DSDM Atern deployment phase will establish products that are fully tested and ready to go live. It also provides a major review of the increment, to apply learning to future timeboxes.

ITIL service transition involves the following ITIL activities:

- Transition planning and support
- Release and deployment management
- Service validation and testing
- Evaluation (of the effects of the service change).

There is a considerable overlap between ITIL's service transition and DSDM Atern deployment – although the scope of service transition is wider, also covering early life support of the live product (see Figure 11.1 for a mapping of this).

Service transition has already had input at the initiation (Initiating a Project) stage, providing direction to planning and scheduling releases, assessing risks and impacts of the transition, and ensuring that time is given to the necessary work of transitioning the service into live operation.

9.4.3 Releasing Features 1 and 2 into the live environment

The release is numbered in the forward schedule of change. It should have a go-live checklist, which lists the elements of organizational importance to handover and the roles and responsibilities assigned for sign-off (acceptance). This can be used to obtain formal sign-off (a good governance practice), but is also a good quality check to ensure that all required aspects have been completed.

9.4.4 Activities from Closing a Project

Some of the activities in the PRINCE2 Closing a Project process will happen repeatedly in an incremental delivery project, possibly as much as once per timebox, rather than just at the close of a project. Closing a Project includes the handover of products to customers and service operation, and the evaluation of the project itself. The PRINCE2 benefits review plan defines how and when to measure achievement of a project's benefits. This needs to take into account the effects of incremental releases, which change the environment being measured.

9.5 HINTS AND TIPS

Since Octagrid has not yet completed Timebox 2, the following suggestions, gathered from more experienced companies, may help it!

- Baseline (version control) before you implement both the new release and the current systems, to allow roll-back and to make benefits measurement possible.
- Have good, pre-tested back-out plans in case the release fails!
- Create a new timebox for early life support so that the success of the release itself can be evaluated separately from the success and completion of the early life support.
- Allow enough time for installation and testing of the infrastructure, for data cleansing, data conversion, data loading, training, and the deployment of documentation and procedures to users.
- Create an organizational go-live checklist per increment, including a responsibility matrix for development, test, release to production, and full production sign-off.
- Set up and pre-test controlled testing and training environments.
- Ensure that team plans account for work and products needed for the release.
- Testing should occur throughout all timeboxes, but there is still some to do at the end.
- Automate the testing, particularly regression testing. Some tests will need to run multiple times.
- Allow time in the plans to transfer, deploy and retire old services, and for early life support.

- Arrange facilitated workshops to review release and, later, early life support and handover to service operation.
- Use ITIL service transition staff to guide change release. ITIL has tips for leading the change and avoiding employee shock (see *Service Transition*).

9.6 CONCLUSION

In this chapter we have considered the complexities of delivering a project incrementally, supporting newly released elements of service whilst maintaining progress on the project. The successful approach to this depends on clearly defined responsibilities, but also on collaborating as a team. Clear plans and continued daily stand-ups are still needed. Respect for the skills of each other's areas is paramount and can only be achieved by increased understanding of the issues in each area. Cross-training of skills is beneficial.

The complexities of frequent deliveries are offset by the relatively smaller size of each release, which tends to make the change easier. It is the frequency of releases that allows the opportunity to improve and perfect the process. Some organizations can deploy to 'live' daily – they just have to become good at it! The real reasons, however, for this regular deployment, are the early release of business value and the opportunity to learn and improve the product. This makes it all worthwhile!

10

Operate!

10 Operate!

In this chapter we look at the results of Octagrid's first incremental delivery of the combined project. You will learn:

- The pitfalls of incremental delivery and how to avoid them
- The benefits of incremental delivery
- How to use a retrospective.

10.1 INTRODUCTION

The COMMANDO project has now completed Timebox 2 (a four-week timebox) and delivered Features 1 and 2. We now turn our attention to Timebox 3, where the first increment of the project is in live operation. This phase highlights some of the potential pitfalls of incremental delivery and, in addition, performs a retrospective of the project so far.

10.2 TIMEBOX 3 – NOT A TYPICAL DEVELOPMENT TIMEBOX

The solution development team has just started Timebox 3, a four-week timebox (Figure 9.1 shows an extract of the plan). In Timebox 3, there is a potentially confusing mix of work to be done. When service transition releases a new product into the live environment, it treats this as a pilot for an agreed period of time and continues to support it, alongside service operation. This helps to provide a smooth handover. Depending upon the project, this pilot may involve the new and old services running in parallel for a while – and this will put extra work on many roles during this period. In addition, the 'big-bang' approach (implementing the whole change at once) may be considered too risky. Therefore, a phased approach could be taken – implementing a few sites at a time, or a few features at a time. During this pilot, service transition staff are very busy in their support of the service desk and in managing the introduction of change (for which ITIL provides guidance in *Service Transition*).

The transition should be made easier by the way in which roles were allocated to the project from the outset. The operations coordinator from the solution development team is a senior service desk operative who knows the product well, having been involved in its development, and is on hand to offer help and advice. The systems integrator from the solution development team has had a similar involvement, and the two roles have collaborated on the production of deployment plans. However, the project needs these individuals back in the solution development team to begin work on the next new feature and, therefore, a conflict of demands will arise.

Similarly, the business ambassadors would also experience a resource conflict because, as well as fulfilling their roles within the solution development team, they also need to support their peers in the business area where the release had been made. In fact, the whole solution development team needs to be on hand to fix any errors, bugs or failures that are likely to arise from the release – they, too, will experience conflicts in demands for their time.

In the COMMANDO project, the team had anticipated that it would be difficult to resource the building of Feature 3 immediately after the release of Features 1 and 2. This resourcing problem would continue into the next timebox too, when scheduled service transition involvement in early life support would clash with service transition's and ambassador users' involvement in the next phase of development. The plan has, however, been built to expect less than 100% of the amount of time each role has given to the project in the first increment (a sensible move!). The team has resolved to keep metrics for the level of commitment of the project resources needed to support the pilots and early life support, to ensure that sufficient time is allowed for this in future projects.

Reassuringly, the first two weeks of pilot working show fewer errors than previous project experience had led the team to expect. The solution development team has already removed many of these errors by testing throughout the process, from both business and technical perspectives (this is typical of a DSDM Atern project with a solution development team made up of the right mix of skills).

10.3 A RETROSPECTIVE

One of the first tasks in Timebox 3 is to hold a retrospective (or review workshop). DSDM Atern uses facilitated workshops as a means of collaborative communication and to produce required outputs. The retrospective is a facilitated workshop that looks back on a recent event (in this case the first delivery into live) and assesses what went well and what could be improved. This should involve the solution development team and other key stakeholders as necessary. The retrospective should have a clear agenda to establish:

- What was done well
- What could be done better
- What the next timebox should work on.

The retrospective should have a clear goal and an atmosphere that is conducive to honesty.

10.3.1 Octagrid's retrospective on Timebox 1

The project board, key stakeholders from the user and supplier groups, the project manager and the solution development team were all present at the retrospective on Timebox 1. Half a day was set aside and an independent facilitator brought in to get the best out of the session.

The link between this workshop and the Managing a Stage Boundary process quickly became evident. The project board wanted to use the retrospective to support its end stage assessment and would not officially release the budget for the second stage of the project until after the retrospective. This caused some delay but, fortunately, in a timebox that had allowed considerable time for support of the pilot, not all of which was needed.

10.3.2 The agenda

The agenda for the retrospective included the following items:

1 Introduction to the plan and where we are now

2 Demonstration of the released product with real data (many demonstrations had been seen before but not the live, released version)

3 Review of the project:

- What we want to keep (what went well)
- What we want to try (a positive slant on what went badly, and how we would like to change it)

4   Next steps for the plan.

In addition to a list of 'keep' and 'try' ideas, an action list and an issues list emerged as the workshop products.

10.3.3 A sample of the workshop outputs

There were many outputs from the workshop, but the top few from each category were:

- Keep (things that worked well):
  - Daily stand-ups
  - Collaborative approach
  - MoSCoW prioritization
  - Visible plans
  - Visible common glossary
  - Visible common roles and responsibilities
  - Celebration of successes
  - Training
  - Modelling the elements of the solution from a user perspective.
- Try (replacements for things that did not work well):
  - Change the consultants' commission scheme whilst they are working on projects (they stopped turning up to workshops at one point because, by spending 50% of their time on the project, they were losing sales commission)
  - Video conferencing and a shared collaborative area online would have helped
  - Try a shorter timebox pattern: four weeks may be too long to keep control of progress, and any longer would lose momentum
  - Name the increments by referring to the related feature set – it became confusing referring to Timebox 2, Increment 2 etc.
  - Take facilitated workshops, timeboxing and

MoSCoW back into any ITIL group situations (CAB, problem resolution groups etc.).

10.4 POST-IMPLEMENTATION REVIEW AND BENEFITS REVIEW

The post-implementation review may include both a review of the project and a review of benefits achieved. Depending upon the project, these may be run at the same time, or separately. The benefits review can start as soon as the business value can be measured, which may even be during the project. PRINCE2 and DSDM Atern endorse the planning of a benefits review during the change project.

The reviews are typically done using facilitated workshops to engage and include appropriate stakeholders. In the case of Octagrid, one review workshop had been scheduled for three months after the final deployment and it has been agreed that benefits will continue to be reviewed at regular intervals during live service operation, in line with ITIL's continual service improvement.

10.5 CONCLUSION

The first incremental delivery of the project was a success for Octagrid. In incremental delivery, it is important that you are aware of the potential conflict of resources between the newly released increment of the service and the continuing project. This is mitigated by careful and realistic planning.

The implementation of an incremental, agile project is typically smoother than a traditional waterfall approach because:

- Key users are already better trained, having

been involved throughout. This is similarly true for service design, service operation and service transition.

- Business ambassadors become true advocates of the change, because they have been involved throughout.

- The end result is more likely to better meet real business needs and the needs of those supporting the service because they have been involved in the project and can ensure that their requirements are included and prioritized. Furthermore, the approach allows for new requirements to be incorporated without increasing cost and time.

- A smaller amount is being deployed at any one release, simplifying the adaptation to change and reducing risk. This enables lessons to be learned along the way, and the product to evolve during its production.

This is where we leave the Octagrid project. COMMANDO is moving towards its final incremental delivery, with a clear measure of the velocity at which the team can work and visibility of the progress made thus far (by completed, usable 'chunks' of the service). Project sponsorship has been kept well informed and can be confident of a timely delivery, with MoSCoW prioritization ensuring that business value is delivered regularly, on time and on budget. Planning for the post-project party has already begun!

The next chapter will bring together what we have learned so far, and offer a full roadmap for implementing DSDM Atern, ITIL and PRINCE2 together.

The sum of
the parts –
the roadmap

11

11 The sum of the parts – the roadmap

In this chapter, you will learn:

- How ITIL, PRINCE2 and DSDM Atern fit together
- Common areas between the three approaches
- A roadmap for using the three approaches together
- Key tips.

11.1 SETTING THE SCENE

We will look at the elements of PRINCE2, ITIL and DSDM Atern and select the best features of each approach to create a roadmap. This roadmap covers the journey through a project, using the culture and techniques of DSDM Atern within an ITIL business-as-usual setting of supporting services.

11.2 HOW TO USE ALL THREE APPROACHES TOGETHER – THE ROADMAP FOR THE COMBINED PROJECT AND BEYOND

In this section, advice and guidance is given on how to build the combined project, process by process, using the PRINCE2 processes as the primary framework and integrating the other approaches into this.

This is intended to be a practical guide and should be tailored to each organization and project. The elements of the three approaches have been kept separate, so that the combined use of any two of the three is also easy to extract.

A roadmap is shown in Figure 11.1. This diagram aligns each PRINCE2 process with the ITIL disciplines and the DSDM Atern phases.

The quality gateways at the bottom of the roadmap diagram are typical points where investment and project approval decisions are made or reaffirmed. The diagram shows an illustrative project with several incremental releases into the live environment (as recommended by DSDM Atern), followed by ITIL periods of pilot and early life support (warranty period).

We look first at combining the roles and team structures. Then each process within the project lifecycle (and beyond) is considered, giving contributions from each approach and tips on how to successfully combine the product sets.

11.2.1 The combined roles and team structures

11.2.1.1 Governance-level roles

The PRINCE2 project management team roles and responsibilities are taken as a template for the governance roles of our combined project and overlaid with elements of the DSDM Atern and ITIL roles, where these can add value. The governance-level roles are shown in Figure 11.2 – the same as Figure 7.3, which was used to illustrate the combined roles in the Octagrid scenario.

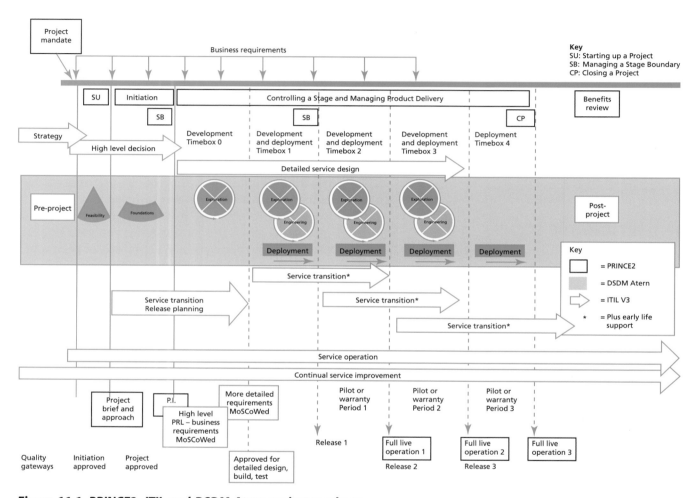

Figure 11.1 PRINCE2, ITIL and DSDM Atern project roadmap

When allocating governance-level roles, consider the following hints and tips:

■ The project board needs to include ITIL representation from both customer (user) and supplier perspectives. This can either be specifically in the roles of senior supplier and senior user, or as members of the groups supporting these roles. The aim is to keep the project board small in size and therefore one senior user and one senior supplier, each backed by a group of representatives, is preferable. Representation from all five service management disciplines is needed in these groups, although there does not usually need to be a separate person for each, and the numbers involved should be kept small. The key customer and supplier areas are:

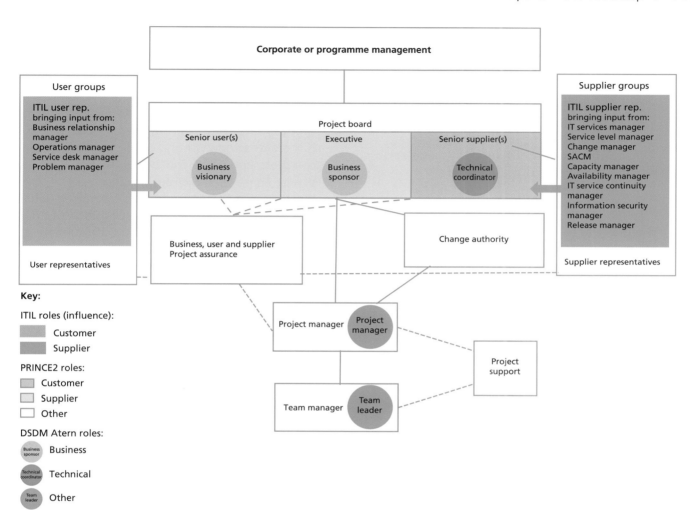

Figure 11.2 Project management team structure – governance roles

- Key customer areas:
  - Service desk (supportability requirements)
  - Continual service improvement (metrics and reporting requirements)
  - Service operation (maintainability requirements)

- Key supplier areas:
  - Capacity management (capacity and infrastructure constraints)
  - Availability management (availability constraints)
  - Supplier management (contractual constraints)

- IT service continuity management (business continuity agreements and constraints)
- Service level management (SLAs in place, OLAs negotiated)
- Change management (change constraints)
- Release management (release scheduling constraints)
- Information security (security regulations and constraints)
- Service asset and configuration management (standards and constraints)

The business relationship manager for the new or changed service will need to be identified early and will input to the acceptance criteria for products; the IT finance manager will input to the business case and will have service-cost-of-ownership reporting requirements.

- Service management should be involved throughout the project, from the outset. The incremental delivery culture reinforces the need for this involvement at all stages of the project.
- ITIL roles are business-as-usual roles. The ITIL representatives will adopt project roles for the duration of the project – for example, the capacity manager may be the best person to assume the project role of technical coordinator in certain types of project.
- The change authority for a project will usually be a different body from the ITIL CAB or ECAB, but the practices used for ITIL change control should not conflict with those for projects.
- Project and ITIL configuration management standards should be aligned, to allow for the easy handover of products into live use.
- When PRINCE2 roles and responsibilities are used, it is with reference to the agile culture of DSDM Atern – for example, project assurance

must understand the impact of its activities on the timeboxed plan and should ensure that these are taken account of during timebox planning so that they do not cause unexpected delay. It is far more helpful to be involved in regular, informal prototype demonstrations of a timeboxed product during the timebox in which it is created than waiting until the product is complete and ready for formal review.

- Where there is an overlap of roles from PRINCE2 and DSDM Atern, it is recommended that the PRINCE2 roles and responsibilities are used, enhanced by elements of DSDM Atern.
- The DSDM Atern business sponsor is the PRINCE2 executive. The size and scope of the project determine where the business visionary and technical coordinator sit within the PRINCE2 hierarchy. On a small project, the visionary role can be combined with the role of executive or senior user; the technical coordinator role can be combined with the role of senior supplier or may be a separate role, performing the tasks of a technical architect to several solution development teams. The business visionary and technical coordinator are very hands-on roles. On a large project, or on one with very senior sponsorship, these roles may be at management levels beneath project board level. However, the link of the vision to project board level must be established.

11.2.1.2 Solution development team roles

At team level, the solution development team roles and responsibilities from DSDM Atern are taken as a template, and ITIL skills are added. At this level, PRINCE2 does not offer specific additional roles below the team manager. Project assurance and the project manager link governance to team level.

The solution development team is a mixed-skill team. All team members, including business roles, have responsibilities in the project and no one is an 'invited guest'! Members must be properly resourced to the project with sufficient availability to do the work required by the project.

Figure 11.3 (which is the same as Figure 7.4, used to illustrate solution development team roles in the Octagrid scenario) shows how the DSDM Atern team is made up of business and solution development skills. Additional roles have been added to cover the required ITIL involvement and

to indicate the involvement, at this level, of project assurance (also shown at the governance level).

ITIL skills from the service design, service transition and service operation disciplines are required in the solution development team. These ITIL skills bring both requirements (e.g. service operation has certain needs in order to be able to support the system) and constraints (e.g. capacity management may place certain constraints on the design of the system and the performance it can achieve) and will have an impact, in particular, upon the non-functional (performance) and reporting

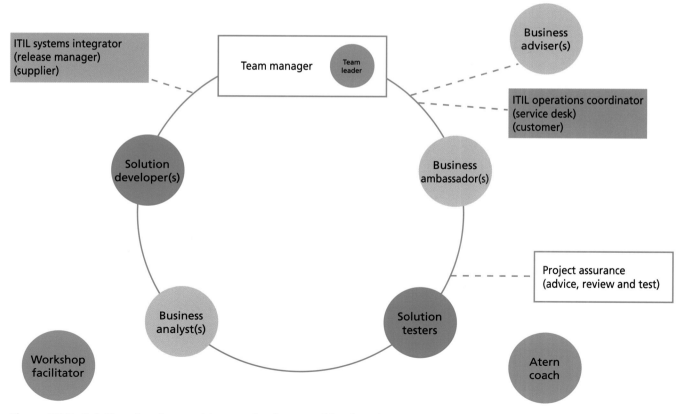

Figure 11.3 Solution development team roles in a combined project

aspects of the product. Two new team roles are proposed with a focus from both customer (user) and supplier sides – operations coordinator (user-focused) and systems integrator (supplier-focused, probably a release manager). These roles need to be carefully defined at solution development team level to ensure that the requirements and constraints are included effectively, and without increasing each team's size beyond the recommended seven (plus or minus two). Multiple small teams may, of course, operate.

In ITIL, the business roles of super user and mentor are recognized by service operation. Ideally, business ambassadors will become super users and mentors once the service is in live operation.

There can be several solution development teams operating at any point in time, each responsible for a different increment of delivery. The systems integrator, operations coordinator, technical coordinator, visionary, business advisers and project assurance may operate across several teams. Plans should be kept visible to all teams throughout the project to facilitate the movement of personnel between teams without jeopardising timebox deadlines. The work related to each role must be visible in the timeboxed plans to ensure that all time is properly resourced.

The solution development team must be empowered by the project board, and any limits on this empowerment should be clear from the outset. One typical element of team empowerment is the ability to de-scope agreed 'should have' and 'could have' requirements without authorization. If empowerment is restricted, the effectiveness of the agile approach is jeopardized.

Management needs to trust the solution development team more than it would in a traditional project. However, the rewards are great – the DSDM Atern project delivers! The risk is mitigated by the frequent delivery of completed, valuable and business-focused products. Completed products are the best measure of progress.

Once the service is in operation, the project roles are decommissioned and the ITIL roles are the only ones remaining in relation to the delivered service. However, the DSDM Atern agile culture can continue into service management.

11.3 WORKING THROUGH THE ROADMAP

Table 11.1 is a quick reference to a roadmap for using the three approaches together. The emboldened elements are the recommended ones to use when combining the approaches; non-emboldened elements are supporting guidance, valuable in combining the approaches. Only key elements are shown. Detailed guidance is given in section 11.4, and Table 11.3 shows where to look for further information on key topics and themes.

Table 11.1 A quick reference for the roadmap

Detailed section	Project phase	Element to use	PRINCE2	DSDM Atern	ITIL
11.4.1	**Pre-project**	Process/discipline	**Starting up a Project**	Pre-project, feasibility	Service strategy Service design CSI
		Roles	Project board Project manager User/supplier groups	Business visionary Technical coordinator	Representatives of ITIL Stakeholders on the project board or in user/supplier groups
		Key products	Project mandate (input) Project brief Initiation stage plan	Feasibility prototype Project approach questionnaire	Service design package (very high-level)
		Main techniques	Product-based planning Business case Risk	Modelling Prototyping MoSCoW Facilitated workshops	
11.4.2	Directing a Project	Process/discipline	**Directing a Project**		Service strategy
		Roles	**Project board**		
		Key products	**Authorization to proceed**		
		Main techniques		**MoSCoW** **Facilitated workshops**	
11.4.3	Initiation	Process/discipline	**Initiating a Project (and Managing a Stage Boundary)**	Foundations	Service strategy Service design Service transition Service operation CSI

Table 11.1 A quick reference for the roadmap *continued*

		Roles	Project board Project manager Project assurance	Business visionary Technical coordinator Solution development team (for estimating)	Representatives of ITIL Stakeholders on the project board or in the user/supplier groups
		Key products	PID Stage plan (timeboxed)	Foundations Prioritized requirements list Solution prototype PAQ revisited	Service design package (but high-level)
		Main techniques	Product-based planning Business case Risk Quality Quality review	Timeboxing MoSCoW Facilitated workshops Prototyping Modelling	
11.4.4	Running the project and delivery	Process/discipline	Controlling a Stage, Managing Product Delivery, Managing a Stage Boundary (parts of Closing a Project)	Exploration Engineering Deployment	Service transition Service operation
		Roles	Project board Project manager Project assurance User and supplier groups	Business visionary Technical coordinator Solution development team	ITIL-specific roles on the project board, user/supplier groups and the solution development team Other service transition and operation roles
		Key products	Highlight reporting Operations and customer sign-offs (increments)	Working (and deployed) increments	Service transition package SLAs, OLAs and UCs

		Main techniques	Change control/ issue handling	Daily stand-ups Iterative development Prototyping MoSCoW Facilitated workshops Retrospectives Agile testing concepts	ITIL testing and piloting
11.4.5	Managing a Stage Boundary	Process/discipline	Managing a Stage Boundary, Directing a Project		
		Roles	Project board Project manager Project assurance User and supplier groups	Business visionary Technical coordinator Solution development team with the ITIL-related roles of operations coordinator and systems integrator	ITIL-specific roles on the project board and in the solution development team
		Key products	End stage report Next stage plan	Working increment	
		Main techniques		Retrospectives	
11.4.6	Closing a Project and early life support	Process/discipline	Closing a Project	Deployment	Service transition Service operation
		Roles	Project manager Project board All stakeholders	Solution development team with the ITIL-related roles of operations coordinator and systems integrator	Other service transition and operation roles
		Key products	Operations and customer sign-offs	Deployed increments	Service transition package

Table 11.1 A quick reference for the roadmap *continued*

		Main techniques		Iterative working	Early life support
				Timeboxing	ITIL guidance
				Prototyping	
				MoSCoW	
				Facilitated workshops	
				Retrospectives	
				Modelling	
11.4.7	Live running	Process/discipline			Service operation
					CSI
		Roles			ITIL roles
		Key products			ITIL guidance
		Main techniques		Iterative working	Detailed ITIL guidance from all disciplines
				Timeboxing	
				Prototyping	
				MoSCoW	
				Facilitated workshops	
				Retrospectives	
				Modelling	
11.4.8	Benefits review	Process/discipline		Post-project	Service operation
					CSI
		Roles	Executive	Business visionary	ITIL stakeholders
			Project manager	Technical coordinator	Business users of the service
			Project stakeholders	All stakeholders	
		Key products	Benefits review plan (input)	Benefits assessment	
			PID		
			Business case		
		Main techniques		Facilitated workshops	

11.4 DETAILED GUIDANCE

The section numbers in the left-hand column of Table 11.1 correspond to the relevant sections that follow. These sections give more detail on the information contained in the table, and take the project from start to close (and beyond!), offering guidance for each process.

The PRINCE2 framework and terminology is generally taken as the template, with elements of ITIL and DSDM Atern added to this.

11.4.1 Pre-project

11.4.1.1 PRINCE2 Starting Up a Project

The PRINCE2 process of Starting Up a Project is a pre-project process and includes:

- Establishing the terms of reference and the approach to the project
- Defining the roles of the project management team and appointing suitable individuals
- Creating an outline business case
- Planning the initiation stage.

11.4.1.2 ITIL contribution

At this stage of the project, consider the contribution that ITIL can make to the PRINCE2 Starting up a Project process:

- The ITIL disciplines recognize a project lifecycle through service design and service transition, and a handover to service operation after a warranty period involving a pilot and early life support. The ITIL elements should not be seen as separate from the development project.
- In appointing the project board, consider ITIL involvement at senior supplier and senior user levels, or in user and supplier groups.

- The project brief should align with service strategy and service design. The project approach should take account of IT infrastructure strategy and the plans for capacity management and financial management. The project objectives, including performance goals, should reflect current SLAs, where appropriate. Customer quality expectations should include ITIL service transition, service operation and continual service improvement needs. The project product description within the project brief must incorporate service management acceptance criteria. The outline business case and outline project plan need to be feasible, in line with the service portfolio and the forward schedule of change.
- ITIL resources should be included at the initiation stage plan.

Additional input from ITIL includes:

- Service level agreements (SLAs), operational level agreements (OLAs) and underpinning contracts (UCs) identified in the service portfolio. These will be useful in setting early expectations and acceptance criteria.
- The service knowledge management system (SKMS) and known error database, which have useful data to add to the lessons learned actively sought in Starting up a Project.

11.4.1.3 DSDM Atern contribution

The DSDM Atern lifecycle phases pre-project and feasibility map to this process and will influence it in the following ways:

- The outline project plan will be timeboxed at a high level. The initiation stage plan will be a timeboxed plan.

■ The outline business case will show scope tolerance, linked to MoSCoW prioritization and the zero time tolerance imposed by timeboxing. How the loss of 'could have' and 'should have' functionality will affect the business case should also be illustrated.

Additional input from DSDM Atern includes:

■ DSDM Atern focuses on early delivery of increments of business-valuable working product and measurement of progress by completed, business-valuable products. Furthermore, time, quality and cost are fixed, and scope tolerance is by prioritization using MoSCoW criteria. Benefit tolerance has some flexibility, but in line with the business case.

■ A 'do enough and no more' (80:20) approach will keep this phase short and the documentation necessary but concise.

■ The project approach questionnaire should be used to help to establish the agile culture.

■ A feasibility prototype will help to establish a clear, shared vision.

■ A facilitated workshop for project kick-off will establish a shared vision and obtain agreement and buy-in from the project management team and key stakeholders.

■ A facilitated workshop is recommended for initial stakeholder identification and risk/opportunity identification.

■ Facilitated workshops will contribute to the effectiveness of supplier and user groups.

11.4.2 Directing a Project

11.4.2.1 PRINCE2 Directing a Project

The first formal Directing a Project activity for the project board is to decide whether to authorize initiation of the project. ITIL and DSDM Atern have no parallel for Directing a Project. Briefing of the project board in their PRINCE2, DSDM Atern and ITIL responsibilities will be necessary. Further information on project board activity can be found in the PRINCE2 publication *Directing Successful Projects with PRINCE2*.

Other Directing a Project activities are related to stage authorizations and exceptions, ad hoc advice and project closure.

Directing a Project creates no management products but approves several, giving the project authorization to start, continue and, finally, to authorize closure.

11.4.2.2 ITIL contribution

The ITIL representation within the project management team will have clear requirements for an operable, maintainable product. The project board must typically operate within the bounds of service strategy. An executive briefing for the project board in ITIL service management may be necessary.

11.4.2.3 DSDM Atern contribution

The agile culture of the project means that as part of the authorizations by the project board, it will also be authorizing the different culture of an agile project. Project board members need to understand their increased involvement and decision-making capacities throughout the project – compared to a non-agile project. The project board needs to appreciate that its decisions have to be made in a very timely way so that the benefits of early delivery are not undermined. An executive briefing for the project board may be needed to convey the benefits of the agile approach and to establish an understanding of the cultural differences. The PAQ will have been completed by the project board and project manager during Starting up a Project.

Communication with the whole team, including the project board, should be simple and face to face wherever possible. The project manager and the project board should communicate regularly about project progress and this communication will be more effective if it is agile in nature and format – that is, frequent without too many formal reports.

The decisions of the project board need to be timely, and in line with the timeboxed plan; delay may result in functionality being de-scoped.

11.4.3 Initiation

11.4.3.1 PRINCE2 Initiating a Project

The PRINCE2 process of Initiating a Project is part of the PRINCE2 'controlled start', which leads to project authorization.

The key activities are:

- Preparing strategies for risk management, quality management, configuration management and communication management
- Setting up progress controls (stages, reporting)
- Creating a more detailed project plan
- Refining the business case
- Assembling the project initiation documentation (PID) to present to the project board for authorization for the project to begin.

This is accompanied by the first run of Managing a Stage Boundary to create a detailed plan for the first stage of technical work (see section 11.4.5).

ITIL, DSDM Atern and PRINCE2 all give advice and guidance on risk, quality, and change and configuration management. PRINCE2 offers the quality review technique and both PRINCE2 and DSDM Atern give advice on plans and agree on the concept of product-based planning (although the more detailed guidance is in PRINCE2).

The project board has already been established in the pre-project phase (Starting up a Project). Project assurance and change authority may be delegated. The solution development team roles need to be identified and, where possible, allocated here within initiation (see section 11.4.3.3).

The standard PRINCE2 management products here are:

- Risk management strategy and risk register
- Configuration management strategy and issue register
- Quality management strategy and quality register
- Communication management strategy
- Project plan, product descriptions and configuration item records
- Benefits review plan
- PID, including project controls, project management team structure and role descriptions, and a detailed business case.

Adaptations and additions to these are described in sections 11.4.3.2 and 11.4.3.3.

11.4.3.2 ITIL contribution

In a three-approach project, ITIL has an important part to play in Initiating a Project:

- There is significant input from all five ITIL disciplines in Initiating a Project. These are represented on the project board, in the user and supplier groups and in the solution development team.

- Service design recognizes the setting up of a project, and defers to the 'application of a formal, structured project methodology' for this (*Service Design*).
- IT financial management will input to the determination and agreement of outline budgets and business benefits and assist with the business case.
- Service design's customer engagement plan will feed into the PRINCE2 communication management plan.
- Service management has definitions for service asset and configuration management standards and for change control, quality and risk. It must be clear in the PRINCE2 strategy products what standards are to be used for the project.
- The project plan and business case must define a project product that is feasible, in line with service strategy and current and planned IT infrastructure.
- The ITIL forward schedule of change (FSC) will influence the project plan. Project releases must be entered into it to ensure planned release dates are feasible.
- The PRINCE2 benefits review plan must be formulated with input from service transition and service operation. Continual service improvement will have requirements for appropriate and comparable metrics.
- A checklist of release criteria and responsibilities for sign-offs must be initiated here (a go-live checklist).
- Service design gives advice on identification of stakeholders, requirements engineering, prioritization, agreement and documentation. It also recommends facilitated workshops and prototyping, although the best advice on this is in DSDM Atern.

11.4.3.3 DSDM Atern contribution

The DSDM Atern lifecycle phase that maps to Initiating a Project is foundations, where firm foundations are established from management, business and solutions perspectives. DSDM Atern can supplement the PRINCE2 process in various ways at this stage:

- A solution prototype is recommended, to establish a shared vision and give early proof of concept. Modelling (diagramming) of the context of the project also helps in this respect.
- An initial solution development team needs to be in operation during Initiating a Project, to be involved in planning and estimating, and for input to the business case.
- Initiating a Project runs in parallel with the first element of Managing a Stage Boundary, for which the solution development team is also needed. Timeboxed team plans are drawn up by the solution development team in parallel with stage plans at this stage.
- DSDM takes a management focus, business focus and solution focus to products. The management and business products are well covered by PRINCE2. The combined project should cross-check these with the product descriptions defined in DSDM Atern to identify any useful additions. The solution-focused products are not covered by PRINCE2's management product set. However, the product breakdown structure should include the solution-focused products, such as solution prototypes and solution review records. To avoid unnecessary documentation, the agile philosophy of 'do enough and no more' should be adopted.
- The products in the product breakdown structure should be MoSCoW prioritized.

- The communication management strategy, which identifies agreed reporting, needs to consider communication from an agile perspective (e.g. facilitated workshops, retrospectives).
- Facilitated workshops can be used to assist with stakeholder analysis, risk identification and the building of the business case and communication plan.
- DSDM Atern gives guidance on requirements engineering, prioritization, facilitated workshops and prototyping.

11.4.4 Running the project and delivery

11.4.4.1 PRINCE2 Controlling a Stage/ Managing Product Delivery

This is the 'controlled progress' element of a PRINCE2 project (Controlling a Stage), plus the link to building the solution (Managing Product Delivery). Where incremental delivery is planned, elements of Closing a Project, for operational handover, also have an influence here. These are considered in more detail in section 11.4.6.

There are two distinct elements to Controlling a Stage:

- Normal working, handing out work to teams and receiving completed work
- Handling issues and changes.

ITIL and DSDM Atern also have approaches to handling issues and changes, but it is recommended that the PRINCE2 approach is adopted.

Managing Product Delivery is responsible for:

- Accepting the work

- Getting it done and completed to the level specified in the work package (tested and signed off, possibly even implemented)
- Notifying its completion.

The standard PRINCE2 management products for Controlling a Stage and Managing Product Delivery should be used:

- Stage plan, team plan
- Work package, product descriptions, configuration item records
- Quality register
- Highlight report, checkpoint report (although this may be face to face)
- Issue register, issue report, exception report
- Risk register, lessons log, daily log.

Adaptations and additions to these products are described in sections 11.4.4.2 and 11.4.4.3.

11.4.4.2 ITIL contribution

ITIL's service transition activities will occur repeatedly in an incremental delivery project, possibly as frequently as every timebox within a stage, but typically where one management stage is a delivery increment. This potentially places live delivery and early life support within Controlling a Stage/Managing Product Delivery. Service transition is described in more detail in section 11.4.6.

It is likely that the project board would direct a stage boundary to take place just after a major release.

ITIL's service design activities will occur repeatedly, typically within every timebox of a stage. Key outputs from ITIL's contribution to this process include:

- The service design package (from service design). This contains a full requirements specification for the design of the service. This is a useful document. However, in our agile project, an incremental approach is needed, with the initial production of a high-level prioritized statement of requirements followed by the emergence of more detail, timebox by timebox.

- The service transition package (from service transition). This should still be used but, once again, in an incremental way – it will emerge as a high-level view initially and then in 'chapters' rather than one issue of a single document.

The influence of ITIL means that work packages would need to cover the service management work. These would be related to products in the product breakdown structure, defined in Initiating a Project.

11.4.4.3 DSDM Atern contribution

The Controlling a Stage process in PRINCE2 provides a controlled break between the project manager and the team, or teams, producing products, whilst work packages form the agreement for work to be done within time, cost and quality tolerances. The agile approach, on the other hand, is more collaborative. However, DSDM Atern still maintains very tight control by the use of timeboxing and daily stand-ups. These DSDM Atern features should be added here to strengthen Controlling a Stage.

The DSDM lifecycle phases of exploration, engineering and deployment map onto the Managing Product Delivery process. They add significantly to that process, detailing the work and team involvement in taking a product from initial analysis and design through to live operation. In particular, the exploration, engineering and deployment phases contribute to Managing Product Delivery in the following ways:

- Work packages operate well with timeboxes, since they are complete and testable pieces of work, with acceptance criteria. Typically, the relationship would be one work package per timebox, per team – although it could be many complete work packages per timebox.

- When they are well run, daily stand-up meetings are more informative than documented checkpoint reports. However, highlight reports are usually still needed as the project board communication.

- Prototyping and facilitated workshops are effective during timeboxes.

- The tester role within the team allows an independent but continual check on the validity of products being produced. There is a potential difficulty in bringing in project assurance to test products, as the team (users and developers) are empowered to build and modify scope within agreed limits – late review can detrimentally affect the timeboxes. If project assurance is aware of the agile process, then this can be managed effectively.

- As Figure 7.4 shows, the solution development team comprises whatever skills it needs to accomplish the work package. The team size is small (seven, plus or minus two), which impacts the way work packages are built by the project manager. These teams comprise mixed business and technical skills. It is not recommended that release teams operate separately from build teams.

11.4.5 Managing a Stage Boundary

11.4.5.1 *PRINCE2 Managing a Stage Boundary*

This is part of the 'controlled progress' element of a PRINCE2 project, and provides a formal review point for the project board to decide whether to continue funding the project or not.

In an incremental delivery project, ITIL's service design and service transition activities will occur repeatedly within a stage.

It is likely that the project board would require a stage boundary after any major release, in addition to other important decision points.

The key elements of Managing a Stage Boundary are concerned with:

- Planning the next stage of the project
- Updating all relevant documentation (project plan, business case etc.)
- Reporting on the end of a stage and the progress made
- If the stage has breached its tolerances, potentially producing an exception plan.

Managing a Stage Boundary is a major strength of PRINCE2. Neither ITIL nor DSDM has an equivalent, although DSDM has a similar potential to make a go/no-go decision at the end of every timebox or delivery increment.

The standard PRINCE2 management products to be used during the Managing a Stage Boundary process include:

- New stage plan, updated previous stage plan
- Updated project plan

- Updated Risks, issues, business case, benefits review plan, lessons report, quality register
- Exception plan
- End stage report.

Adaptations and additions to these are described in sections 11.4.5.2 and 11.4.5.3.

11.4.5.2 ITIL contribution

In a three-approach project, ITIL can make important contributions at this stage:

- One element of an end stage assessment is to reconsider the constitution of the project teams, including the project board for the stage. Depending upon the intended products of the next stage, changes to ITIL roles in the solution development team, project board and user/supplier groups will be considered.
- The service design package and service transition package, emerging incrementally, will provide useful information. However, keep in mind that working products, rather than documentation, are the primary measure of progress.

11.4.5.3 DSDM Atern contribution

DSDM has valuable contributions to make to the project at this stage:

- Managing a Stage Boundary involves planning: the next stage plan or an exception plan. An agile team must be involved in all planning activity to ensure the creation of realistic timeboxes and informed estimates to which the team can commit.
- Facilitated workshops, with involvement from all stakeholders who have an impact on the plan, are a recommended way of planning.

- If an incremental approach is being followed, the benefits review plan must report actual benefits achieved with products released during the project.
- The DSDM Atern project will embrace change, whilst focusing on the overall consistent project objectives. This may mean considerable change from the PID, and a complete reassessment of the business case in some situations.
- The mechanism for reporting at the end of the stage may, by project board agreement, be informal and could be a presentation or workshop.

11.4.6 Closing a Project and early life support

Closing a Project is the 'controlled close' of a PRINCE2 project, running in parallel to ITIL's service transition and DSDM Atern's deployment. Service transition then takes the product into a warranty period of early life support. However, service transition and deployment may also occur repeatedly during an incremental delivery project, possibly as frequently as every timebox within a stage.

11.4.6.1 PRINCE2 Closing a Project

The key elements of Closing a Project are concerned with:

- Preparing for a planned or premature closure of the project
- Handing over products to customers and service operation
- Evaluating the project method and results
- Recommending that the project be closed.

The standard PRINCE2 management products to be used or updated are:

- Project plan
- Product status account
- Issue register, risk register, quality register, daily log, lessons log
- Draft project closure notification (quality criteria not defined in PRINCE2)
- Additional work estimates (quality criteria not defined in PRINCE2)
- Follow-on action recommendations (quality criteria not defined in PRINCE2)
- Configuration item records
- Benefits review plan
- End project report
- Lessons report
- Acceptance record (quality criteria not defined in PRINCE2).

Adaptations and additions to these are described in sections 11.4.6.2 and 11.4.6.3. Those PRINCE2 products that do not have quality criteria defined, are defined by ITIL's service transition.

It should be noted that the benefits review plan defines how and when to measure achievement of the project's benefits. However, the project will have closed before this review takes place. Thus, this is a document for agreement with, and handover to, ITIL service management. This will ensure that metrics continue to be captured so that the performance before and after the change can be compared, and so that the post-implementation review takes place appropriately.

Section 11.4.3.2 referred to the go-live checklist. This checklist is essential to the smooth transition of a service into live operation, both during and at the end of the project.

11.4.6.2 ITIL contribution

The ITIL disciplines of service transition and early life support are strong additions to PRINCE2 here. Where PRINCE2 and DSDM Atern do not define the exact format of handover documents, ITIL does – a formal service transition package.

Service transition includes:

- Transition planning and support
- Release and deployment management
- Service testing and validation
- Evaluation (of the effects of the service change).

Both service transition and DSDM have significant guidance on testing, including regression testing, which is a major, ongoing part of the testing within an incremental delivery project. Collaboration on testing activity is vital within the solution development team.

Service transition does not end when the PRINCE2 project traditionally ends. The team usually goes on to give early life support to the project's products. In this case, the project closure may be delayed, or a separate project for the early life support set up. This has implications for project budget, for the product breakdown structure of the first project, and for the advance planning of early life support activities.

11.4.6.3 DSDM contribution

The DSDM Atern deployment phase has an impact here – although deployment is not exclusively used for Closing a Project.

The primary purpose of the deployment phase is to move increments of the solution into live usage and act as a review point. This includes training and the provision of documentation for users, and operations and support staff that will be responsible for supporting and maintaining the solution. It should be noted that some of those supporting and using the product are actually in the solution development team, and can act as ambassadors. The business ambassadors will become the super users and mentors recognized by ITIL. The solution developers may form the early life 'snag list' team working alongside service operations.

DSDM has significant guidance on testing (including test-first development). It also has a post-project phase, which gives advice on benefits review.

There is considerable overlap between the objectives of DSDM Atern's deployment phase and ITIL's service transition activities, as highlighted in Table 11.2.

11.4.7 Live running

Both DSDM Atern and PRINCE2 are specifically project approaches. Although the combined project has now closed, the ITIL members of the project team will carry useful agile practices back to their service management roles. If the environment is conducive to this and empowerment is given, these practices will improve the effectiveness of service operations and the other ITIL disciplines.

The service design team is advised to embed the following practices into service management procedures:

- Facilitated workshops for the CAB and ECAB, steering committees, focus groups and other groups where appropriate.
- Use of workshops for retrospectives and 'futurespectives' of work in any area. ITIL service design already suggests using workshops to generate ideas.

Table 11.2 How DSDM Atern's deployment phase and ITIL's service transition activities overlap

Deployment objectives	Deployment (DSDM Atern)	Service transition (ITIL)
To deploy the solution (or increment of it) into the live business environment	Y	Y
To confirm the ongoing performance and viability of the project and re-plan as required	Y	Y
Where applicable, to train the end users of the solution and/or provide necessary documentation to support the live operation of the solution in the business environment	Y	Y
To train and/or provide documentation for operations and support staff who will be responsible for supporting and maintaining technical aspects of the solution	Y	Y
To assess whether the deployed solution is likely to enable the delivery of intended elements of business benefit described in the business case	Y	Y
To formally bring the project to a close	Y	Y
To review overall project performance from a technical and/or process perspective	Y	Y
To review overall project performance from a business perspective	Y	Y

- Modelling is already a practice within ITIL, but a user focus on diagrams will enhance their usefulness as a communication tool. Visual formats, such as pictures and storyboards, can be very helpful.
- Documentation is often used without considering the form in which it is presented or whether all of it is needed, all of the time. A lean, agile attitude to documentation should be encouraged.
- ITIL actively encourages extensive tool support for the service management processes (SKMS, incident management etc.). This is good advice for managing the complexity of the modern IT infrastructure. However, the agile approach of sometimes using face-to-face and informal communication must not be overlooked!
- Daily stand-up meetings are a useful progress check and motivator to any team with a deadline to meet.
- Timeboxing will add focus to any task or process.
- An iterative approach to most aspects of work can be a real enabler, and the culture of MoSCoW prioritization can be embedded with the question 'what's the least we can do to get this working effectively?' This is something that incident management already does.

11.4.8 Benefits review

Benefits review starts as soon as the value can be measured, which may be during the project, immediately after the project or several months after the completion of the project. DSDM Atern addresses this in its post-project phase. However, it is ITIL, with continual service improvement (CSI) that has most to offer here. This is not a one-time activity: it needs to be carried out to assess the effectiveness of the project, but it also needs to continue throughout the life of the service, leading to service modification or replacement at some time in the future. CSI, with its seven-step process for feedback and improvement, gives full advice and guidance on this.

11.5 KEY SOURCES OF GUIDANCE

Table 11.3 gives a summary of the key features that each approach can bring to a project. Where there is potential conflict between them, this is commented upon.

Where a 'Y' is shown, the approach has something to offer a project in this area. Up to five Ys indicates more extensive and useful advice. This is a subjective assessment, intended as a visual cue to where to find advice. Where two or three methods are recommended, it is because they all have different and complementary advice to offer. Where there is a choice, a selection has been made on the basis of what would work better in the combined project environment, and should not be taken to mean that the other approaches are deficient in that area.

Table 11.3 Key sources of guidance

	PRINCE2 (2009)	ITIL v3	DSDM Atern v2	Which approach to use in combined projects?	Comment
Key elements of advice for projects:					
Principles	YYY	Y	YYYYY	DSDM Atern	PRINCE2 principles are more procedural than those in DSDM Atern
Roles (organization)	YYYYY	Y	YYYYY	PRINCE2 for governance roles; business visionary and technical coordinator from DSDM Atern; DSDM Atern for solution development Team roles	New project roles for ITIL are proposed in Chapter 11

Table 11.3 Key sources of guidance *continued*

Project lifecycle	YYYYY	YYY	YYYYY	PRINCE2 as the driver, with contributions from DSDM Atern and ITIL	ITIL adds service transition and handover to live running
Other guidance for projects:					
Business case	YYYYY	Y IT strategy level	YYY	PRINCE2 guidance, plus corporate standards for projects	Business and IT strategy should drive project business cases
Quality	YYYYY	YY	YYY	PRINCE2 for projects	ITIL advice is for service operation
Plans/planning	YYYYY	N	YYYYY	PRINCE2 for project and stage plans, incorporating DSDM Atern timeboxing	DSDM Atern also for plans at team level
Risk	YYYYY	YY	YYY	PRINCE2, with a DSDM Atern timeboxed and prioritized approach overlaid	ITIL and PRINCE2 are based on OGC standard guidance on management of risk (M_O_R®)
Change	YYYYY	YYY	YYYYY	PRINCE2 procedures for issues and escalation; DSDM Atern culture of team empowerment around prioritized requirements and 'embracing change'	ITIL change procedures for service operation. These are similar to PRINCE2 procedures
Progress (tolerances)	YYYYY	N	(handled via MoSCoW)	PRINCE2 and DSDM Atern approaches should both be used	Use defined scope tolerance but no time tolerance on a DSDM Atern project
Estimating	N	N	YYY	DSDM Atern	DSDM Atern has useful information to add on agile estimation.

Metrics/measurement	N	YYY	Y	ITIL and DSDM Atern	ITIL includes CSI, which is concerned with metrics capture and interpretation
Management and business-focused products	YYYYY	YYY	YYY	PRINCE2 products should be used as the standard, with an agile approach to lean documentation	
Solution-based products	N	Y	YYYYY	DSDM Atern	ITIL has some useful information on service design packages and service transition to cross-reference
Facilitated workshops	N	Y	YYYYY	DSDM Atern	
MoSCoW prioritization	Y	Y	YYYYY	DSDM Atern	
Iterative development	Y	Y	YYYYY	DSDM Atern	
Timeboxing	N	N	YYYYY	DSDM Atern	
Modelling	Y	Y	YYYYY	DSDM Atern for general guidance; PRINCE2 for product-based planning	ITIL for capacity planning and other business-as-usual modelling
Requirements engineering	N	YYY	YYYYY	DSDM Atern	ITIL service design also has guidance here
Testing	N	YYYY	YYYY	DSDM Atern for agile testing, ITIL for service transition testing levels	
Configuration management	YYYY	YYYYY	YYY	ITIL standards should drive the PRINCE2 configuration management strategy	Projects should be aligned to the configuration management system to be used after delivery

11.6 KEY TIPS FOR COMBINING DSDM ATERN, PRINCE2 AND ITIL

As a final note in this chapter, the following checklist offers key tips for combining the three approaches:

- Beware of culture clashes. DSDM Atern, PRINCE2 and ITIL service management have much in common, but many cultural differences.
- Project sponsorship is essential – this means that the budget holder and champion of the project needs to be the right person, at the right level and with the right availability.
- Remember the cost/time/quality triangle? Flex the functionality, not the time, budget or quality.
- MoSCoW everything – including requirements, testing, deliveries etc.
- Operate continual improvement throughout using daily stand-ups, lessons learned, retrospectives, known errors. Build and use the knowledge base.
- Have change control, but do not prevent change. Allow for evolution and learning.
- Operate configuration management, but ensure that it is not a punitive overhead.
- Test early and continuously.
- Empower teams and encourage them to collaborate, by creating the right environment and employing the right management style.

11.7 CONCLUSION

In our journey to combine three best-practice approaches, we have moved from pre-project, through the project itself and beyond into service operation and continual service improvement.

Individually, PRINCE2, DSDM Atern and ITIL have much to offer. Together, they are a complete, robust approach to the effective and improving provision of IT services to support business needs. The whole is greater than the sum of its parts!

12

Case studies

12 Case studies

12.1 INTRODUCTION

This chapter focuses on the experiences of four organizations, kind enough to talk candidly about their introduction and use of ITIL, PRINCE2 and DSDM Atern for the purposes of this publication. In a series of interviews in 2008 and 2009, the organizations agreed to share their implementation stories so that others may learn from their experiences.

The organizations were specifically chosen to represent the following sectors:

- A large commercial organization (Allied Irish Banks)
- A charity (AQA Examinations Board)
- A local government organization (Hampshire County Council)
- A government department (The Met Office, part of the MOD).

The organizations have all contributed useful hints and tips to guide other organizations as they embark on some, or all, of the journey toward using PRINCE2, DSDM Atern and ITIL.

12.2 ALLIED IRISH BANKS (AIB)

12.2.1 Background information on AIB

AIB is Ireland's largest financial institution, delivering banking services to more than 18 countries worldwide including the United States, Germany, Poland, France and Australia. AIB was incorporated in Ireland in September 1966 as a result of the amalgamation of three long-established banks: the Munster and Leinster Bank (established 1885), the Provincial Bank of Ireland (established 1825) and the Royal Bank of Ireland (established 1836). The AIB Group is a worldwide banking and financial services organization. The Group employs some 25,000 people worldwide.

Within AIB, back-office business operations and information technology are located within a cross-enterprise group called operations and technology (O&T). O&T has more than 4,000 staff, 1,200 of whom work in four main IT areas across Ireland, Poland and Great Britain.

The O&T mission is: 'To create an efficient engine on which the business can rely for the long term.' It strives to deliver operational excellence by meeting customer expectations, mitigating risk, reducing operating cost and being compliant with regulatory requirements. It does this by simplifying processes, implementing common platforms and striving to reduce complexity. The implementation of best-practice approaches to managing and improving IT services is key to the fulfilment of these goals.

12.2.2 Where are they now with ITIL, PRINCE2 and DSDM Atern?

AIB uses tailored versions of DSDM Atern and ITIL and a project and change management approach which reflects elements of PRINCE2. The approaches are discussed in the following sections in the sequence in which they were adopted.

12.2.2.1 DSDM

The bank was a very early adopter of DSDM, recognizing the need to deliver products to market quickly, whilst retaining the right quality and keeping costs within the bounds of the original investment decision for the project. AIB has actively followed the DSDM approach since 1997, inputting to early releases of the method. The bank has chosen to tailor the approach over the years. However, it still retains all of its structure, roles and techniques, whilst having a few additional products and checks added to meet stringent financial and regulatory needs. DSDM was given its own internal identity and 'brand' within the bank, described initially as 'design and build' and later as the solution development lifecycle (SDLC). AIB also incorporated improvements to DSDM as these were made over the years by the DSDM Consortium and has incorporated the latest DSDM Atern principles, practices and techniques into its SDLC.

A key success factor in AIB's adoption of DSDM was the clever way in which AIB introduced it into the organization's practices. Initially, DSDM was implemented in a gradual way, by providing regular and available DSDM Practitioner training, plus introductory awareness sessions, short topic-based 'lunch-bite' sessions and a supporting intranet area for templates and advice. Initially, project managers were able to choose whether to use the approach and how much of it to use, selecting elements of the approach that they found helpful. The uptake was therefore initially slow and organic rather than swift and enforced. However, consistent and supportive senior management sponsorship for the approach was present throughout and this contributed significantly to success. The training was linked to people's performance objectives and individuals

were empowered, via intranet-based tools, to book their own training. Masterclasses were run for champions of the approach and a support team and centre of excellence were established to offer help and advice and even to offer extra resource to support projects, facilitating workshops and performing project health checks. Training courses incorporated 'guest speakers' from within the organization who, rather than talking generically about project success, highlighted individual techniques within the bank's projects which had been used in a particularly effective way. In 2008, the approach was made mandatory for all projects, but by this time all project staff had been trained in the approach and knew the benefits, so most were already using it anyway! There was no resistance as, 'It was now the way we did business.' The setting up of a specialized support team and the creation of internal branding helped to propagate the growth and lead to successful and sustained adoption.

12.2.2.2 PRINCE2

AIB does not use PRINCE2 in its standard form, but has developed an in-house approach to project governance, adopting elements of PRINCE2 and PMI in combination, to form a tailored approach. PRINCE2 provides the process and framework whilst the PMI approach, based on the Project Management Body of Knowledge (PMBOK) provides the techniques and soft-skills aspects. The approach is internally known as the project and change management method (P&CMM). This approach runs as an umbrella to DSDM, with the distinction that the P&CMM manages the 'what' of the project and the DSDM approach covers the 'how'.

In 2002, increased legislation within the banking industry and the impact of SOX (Sarbanes-Oxley) regulations resulted in AIB setting up a large-scale change programme across the AIB Group to strengthen project management and IT service delivery. The project to bring about this change culminated in a more formal approach to running projects, which incorporated governance-based project management from the P&CMM and the agile project delivery elements of the systems development lifecycle (SDLC), which is substantially DSDM Atern. Thus, DSDM Atern and key elements of PRINCE2 now form the core of the mandated way of working on change projects, used by the bank worldwide. The links between the SDLC and P&CMM are built into each of the approaches.

12.2.2.3 ITIL

ITIL was the last element of the journey, introduced between 2007 and 2009, initially with ITIL v2 and then progressing to ITIL v3, a transformation which is still ongoing at the time of writing. AIB succeeded in moving from a situation where it had no formalized service management, (although many legacy processes to manage individual IT services were in place) to receiving the ISO/IEC 20000 certification in December 2007 in Poland and by June 2008 in Ireland.

ITIL implementation was part of a major operations and technology change programme, initiated in 2005 to deliver operational excellence to support AIB's business across all divisions. A programme structure was set up, bringing senior representatives together from every division. ITIL implementation was run as a project within this programme.

The project to introduce ITIL was a high-profile and well-orchestrated initiative which was given a strong identity and codenamed 'Project Olympus', reflecting the mountain which the organization felt it had to climb to achieve successful implementation. The aim of Olympus was to provide a standardized set of IT service management processes, supported by a standard toolkit and the necessary skill set. A cross-divisional IT council was formed to progress the Olympus agenda. Sponsorship for the whole programme was visibly given at CEO level. The Olympus project was set up across three departmental/divisional streams with a senior sponsor for each stream.

The first phase of the project was to get the cross-divisional teams to agree one set of Group-wide service management processes. Initial focus was on six or seven of the key ITIL processes. This evolved into 13 processes and a service management governance framework. A project management office was responsible for the day-to-day running of Project Olympus. Key AIB staff were released to work on the programme, with external staff being brought in to cover normal tasks. External staff, including ITIL experts were also brought in to support the AIB project team.

The project was run under the P&CMM project management approach, with its elements of PRINCE2 and PMI. The DSDM influences were also there through the staff knowledge of the SDLC. Rich communication techniques, including facilitated workshops and simulations, were employed.

Staff were trained in ITIL, with 86% being trained to Foundation level and a number trained to ITIL Manager level. However, training, education and awareness were also reinforced by posters, newsletters, meetings, simulations, demonstrations and a very well-received lunchtime play to illustrate ITIL to people in an innovative and memorable way.

During the implementation, processes were tailored to embed Sarbanes-Oxley key controls and the opportunity was taken to gain ISO 20000 certification as a sign of independent validation of the processes.

AIB has kept metrics to evaluate the effectiveness of ITIL adoption. Based on reduced downtime, fewer service incidents, reduced cost and improvement in the time to resolve incidents, major improvements in services have been seen and they have produced impressive cost savings. The use of a common set of IT service management processes has led to an improved compliance environment, increased service quality and better management of cost and risk.

12.2.3 Order of implementation

DSDM and PRINCE2/PMI, followed by ITIL.

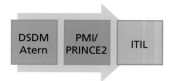

12.2.4 Any specific learning points to share with others?

The following key points emerged in answer to this question:

- ITIL implementation is a significant cultural change, asking people to change the way they work and interact. People need to be shown the benefits before they will change.
- Large-scale change requires visible and continued senior sponsorship.
- The implementation needs to be aligned to a clear business strategy.

- Create an identity (a brand) for introducing the new approach.
- Ensure that working in the new disciplines has a clear career path.
- Communicate continually to all audiences throughout the change, to win hearts and minds.
- Use a variety of communication methods: AIB used posters, email, presentations, simulations, team meetings, articles in the company magazine, AIB-specific games and even theatrical performances at lunchtimes! A comprehensive awareness programme was planned in advance and implemented.
- Sell the benefits, but acknowledge the potential difficulties too.
- There are huge gains in sharing information and experiences across processes and divisions.
- The journey never ends. There is the need for continual improvement.
- The introduction of change takes a lot of resource. Backfill normal roles rather than expecting people to just fit in the change alongside their normal work. Use dedicated roles and responsibilities – consider going for one person, one role.
- Give positive feedback to those making the change. Find something that works well and say 'thank you'!

12.3 THE ASSESSMENT AND QUALIFICATIONS ALLIANCE (AQA)

12.3.1 Background information on AQA

AQA employs approximately 1,050 staff at offices in Manchester, Guildford and Harrogate. It is the largest of the three English examinations boards, awarding 49% of full-course GCSEs and 42% of A levels nationally. In total, candidates take more than 3.5 million examinations with AQA each year. AQA is an independent registered charity; all income is used to run the examinations, and carry out research and development to improve those qualifications and services.

AQA works closely with teachers, schools, colleges, employers, higher education, government and the regulators to promote the smooth running and continuing development of the UK qualifications system to give every learner the opportunity to realize their potential.

12.3.2 Where are they now with ITIL, PRINCE2 and DSDM Atern?

AQA has used PRINCE2 for many years. DSDM Atern has only recently been introduced and the organization has just embarked upon ITIL implementation. The approaches are discussed in the following sections in the sequence in which they were adopted.

12.3.2.1 PRINCE2

PRINCE2 has been in use at AQA since 2003 and is the standard used for all projects. It has been adopted gradually to the point where now all of the PRINCE2 processes are followed, project boards are formed for all projects and most of the management products are in use – in particular, project briefs, project initiation documentation (the PID), highlight reports and exception reports are all used. It is only more recently that the approach has been taken down to team level, but now checkpoint reports are part of the project reporting structure. Projects within AQA are usually relatively short, and thus the idea of management stages is not particularly used – it is more likely that

in a lengthy endeavour, each new element would be treated as a separate project.

PRINCE2 was chosen as a good established method. However, the general feeling in a small organization such as AQA, is that, although rich and well structured, it is complex; it requires a substantial amount of work to implement fully. Templates for the management products are a necessity.

12.3.2.2 DSDM Atern

DSDM Atern has been in use in AQA since 2008 and implementation is still in progress, targeted to specific projects only at the time of writing. Selected techniques have been adopted, in particular MoSCoW prioritization, timeboxing and facilitated workshops, and some significant successes have been reported in the use of these. DSDM Atern is always used within a PRINCE2 framework and the DSDM Atern lifecycle and roles have been tailored to fit with this.

The rollout of DSDM Atern has taken longer than management had expected. It identifies possible reasons for this as the differences in interpretation of the DSDM Atern approach between staff, attributable to the fact that not all project managers and project staff were able to have the appropriate training in the approach.

However, thus far, the business users have welcomed the approach and have stated that they now appreciate the complexity of the development process. They have been keen to be involved in the projects and recognize the benefits of prioritization and user involvement, compared to the waterfall process to which they were accustomed.

12.3.2.3 ITIL

ITIL implementation was in the very early stages in 2009. No information was gathered in this area, due to the newness of the implementation.

12.3.3 Order of implementation

PRINCE2 followed by DSDM Atern, and finally ITIL will be added.

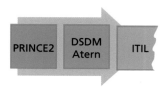

12.3.4 Any specific learning points to share with others?

The following key points emerged in answer to this question:

■ Don't 'reinvent the wheel'. Find out if someone else has the answer, the template or the tool. Find out what templates are already publicly available.

■ Don't try to implement all at once – pick the most beneficial aspects of any method and tailor implementation to your organization and needs.

■ 'Sow the seeds' with people. Communicate via presentations, one-to-one explanations, whatever works. Check understanding regularly, especially with senior management to ensure that it fully understands the concept of managing the scope of a project and that the project may not deliver all of the requirements (except, of course, the must haves)

■ Release planning needs to be given time and be done early:

● Frequent releases increase the complexity and there is impact from several projects all trying to use the same release resources. A matrix is needed to give visibility to each project of other projects' release needs.

● The complexity of releases adds cost. Balance the desire for frequent release with cost and practicality.

● Greater skill is needed by the release and deployment staff and by testers when releases are frequent.

■ Automated testing tools are needed to allow for the increased complexity of regression testing.

■ MoSCoW the defects as well as the requirements – so that the team is always focused on delivering 'must haves'.

■ Consider planning for and scheduling a 'tidy-up' timebox prior to the final release in order to address any defects that have been deferred by the MoSCoW process in previous timeboxes.

■ Not enough time is allowed for deployment, which may take up to 25% of the project time.

■ Requirements capture is problematic and non-functional requirements often emerge very late.

12.4 HAMPSHIRE COUNTY COUNCIL (HCC)

12.4.1 Background information on HCC

Hampshire is the third-largest county in England in terms of population serving some 1.7 million people. It comprises 11 district or borough councils and 251 parish councils. HCC employs around 39,000 people, employed in schools, children's and adult services, environment, recreation and centralized services.

Hampshire County Council's IT services department (HCC IT) supports an annual investment of approximately £6 million in IT-enabled projects. The project support office currently supports all IT-enabled projects and maintains the full list of those projects in progress in the county council (a challenging task in itself!). Project prioritization is service-centric and customer-centric. About 300 people are currently employed in the IT services department, with IT staff in other departments bringing this to between 400 and 500 staff.

12.4.2 Where are they now with ITIL, PRINCE2 and DSDM Atern?

HCC IT uses PRINCE2 for IT-enabled projects; it has adopted ITIL as the basis of its formal service management and is about to embark on the implementation of DSDM Atern to harness agility in these areas. HCC IT has an IT change board and is in the process of establishing a corporate change board. The IT Change Board meets weekly and reviews any proposed changes to the live environment as well as the progress of previous changes: whether they were successful, failed or pulled at the last minute. The approaches are discussed in the following sections in the sequence in which they were adopted.

12.4.2.1 PRINCE2

The implementation of PRINCE2 was a lengthy endeavour, taking place between 2003 and 2006. The driver for adopting PRINCE2 was the desire to improve the way in which projects were run and to give more consistency. It was also driven by an agenda of improving staff recruitment and retention by having industry-recognized best practice in use within HCC IT. It has proved to be the case that this makes IT services 'a good place to work'. It also facilitates projects which involve working with other local authorities and partners as PRINCE2 is a public-sector standard and is also used by commercial suppliers.

The implementation was approached flexibly, with people being given a choice about whether to use it on their projects or not. Within HCC IT, this was considered later to have been much slower and less effective than if implementation had been set up as a project (as with the ITIL implementation) and there had been a level of insistence upon its use within projects.

PRINCE2 was introduced in a tailored way with assistance from an external consultancy and was already in place before the ITIL implementation, meaning that there was internal knowledge to use the project management to treat that as a project.

12.4.2.2 ITIL

Improved delivery of services, better use of resources and a stable base for continual improvement were amongst the key drivers for the implementation of formal service management based on ITIL. Improved control of release and change were also key requirements. The implementation of ITIL within HCC IT was extremely fast, compared to its experiences with PRINCE2 adoption. At the beginning of 2007, HCC IT had no formalized service management framework in place. It did, however, have formal processes in some areas such as incident management and change control. The first step was a gap analysis to take stock of what could be re-used. By early 2008, the organization had achieved full ITIL implementation, and it gained ISO 20000 accreditation in March 2008. The ITIL implementation was run as a PRINCE2 project. This was enabled by the strong awareness of the PRINCE2 method within the ITIL implementation team, as resources were shared between development projects and service management.

It was recorded, in time directly booked to the project, to have taken 6,500 hours to implement ITIL. On a conservative scale, this is around four man-years in 14 months. Added to this, HCC IT opted for a big bang approach, implementing 17 ITIL processes all together (for those who are counting, an overall service management (OSM) responsibility was the 17th process). All processes were in place by November 2007, which makes the statistics even more impressive. HCC IT also achieved ISO 27001 (Security) in March 2008.

The approach was to assign process owners and deputy process owners to each of the ITIL processes. Not all were full time and some of these were natural moves from their usual jobs – for example, the existing help desk manager became the service desk and incident manager. Assignments of process responsibilities that were not a natural move from existing job roles were availability management, capacity management, change management, configuration management, problem management, release management, security management and service level reporting. One downside of using existing staff in existing roles was the reality of people having to implement ITIL in addition to doing their usual day-to-day job. Although they could book time to the ITIL project, the normal job still placed high demands on their time.

The assigned process owners and deputies were tasked with the success of their areas and physical sign-offs were taken from each to say that they had read and understood their responsibilities and the relevant ITIL documentation. This was an unusual step in the culture of HCC IT, but thought

necessary to achieve the challenging targets set for the implementation.

In order to train staff in ITIL, there was widespread use of an ITIL introductory course and many were trained to ITIL Foundation level. However, only a few people were given the full ITIL Service Manager training.

During the implementation of ITIL, there were some issues around the relevance of ITIL to all IT staff, particularly as some development project managers thought ITIL should not affect them, even in the disciplines of change, configuration management and release management. This was addressed by constant communication. The strongest advice to emerge from the implementation team was: 'Communicate! Win hearts and minds! Let people know what's in it for them!'

At the time of writing, ITIL is well embedded. There are still areas for improvement. In particular, release and change management activities are still often left until the end of a project and seen as an overhead and barrier to change; this is being addressed by using the release manager as the interface between the project and all other ITIL processes. In addition, at the start of every project a 'change control' notice is now issued to make all ITIL process owners aware of the start of a project, and the expected timeframe and deliverables. At the end of the project, a release form has to be completed and a business continuity form has to be signed before a change is accepted into the live environment.

The key benefits that have been achieved, attributable to ITIL, are a greater consistency and efficiency in the management of services and tangible cost savings in the number of failed change releases. Service level reporting is better and it can now be recognized when service levels are breached or even under threat, allowing reparative action to be taken. It is also easier to anticipate the impacts of business change and avoid underestimation of capacity requirements. It has highlighted the effects of poorly tested projects – in the past, projects may have been successful in delivering on time but the fact that ongoing maintenance costs of unstable releases had been collected by service provision had been largely unrecognized.

12.4.2.3 DSDM Atern

At the end of 2009, DSDM Atern had not yet been implemented within HCC IT, although strong interest was present following an introductory training session on DSDM Atern and the inclusion of DSDM Atern within business analysis training, to incorporate the agile and iterative approach to requirements capture and management. Future plans include the introduction of DSDM Atern. The 'spirit' is there for incremental development and iterative team working with joint development teams (users and developers), which have already been established for some initiative. One expected benefit of the introduction of DSDM Atern is the breaking down of barriers between roles and greater respect for each other's skills, especially between developers and service management staff.

12.4.3 Order of implementation

PRINCE2, then ITIL. DSDM Atern had not been implemented at the time of writing but was part of future plans.

12.4.4 Any specific learning points to share with others?

The following key points emerged in answer to this question:

- Senior management commitment is needed for implementation and ongoing embedding of the approaches.
- Implement PRINCE2 first. Then you have the project discipline to implement ITIL.
- During implementation, focus on good communication. Let people know why the change is happening, what the benefits are to them, what the implications are for them and the relevance to their job.
- Communicate! Consider the following publicity ideas, they may work for you:
  - An email ITIL quiz with prizes
  - Regular email updates
  - An intranet information site
  - Posters
  - Process owners visited teams and gave short presentations in team meetings.
- During the ITIL implementation project, create publicity and communicate:
  - Right across the project community in IT services
  - To customers as well as IT staff.
- Beware the ITIL myth that release management activities are an excuse for late delivery.
- Take account of problem areas during the development project:
  - Supplier management: how are you controlling the suppliers and what are the implications for service operation later?
  - Continuity management: consider corporate risk and include planning for continuity during the project – the duplication of a data centre, for example

- Configuration management: this needs to be consistent during and after the development project.
- Involve the project office in the implementation project, not just the development project!
- Project boards and executives should understand their responsibilities too. Project managers should, however, understand their responsibility and not expect excessive amounts of time from executives and project boards.
- Joint development can be challenging to resource especially if it demands dedicated allocation of IT resources to projects.
- Terminology becomes confusing, with several approaches being followed. Create a common glossary.
- Always keep a common-sense approach. No method or process should replace this. Don't become obsessed with the method for its own sake. Always ask, 'What is the real problem we are trying to solve?' Understand the problem, benefits, needs and risks.

12.5 THE MET OFFICE

12.5.1 Background information on the Met Office

The Met Office was established in 1854, as a department within the Board of Trade. In 1996, it became part of the Ministry of Defence.

The Met Office employs approximately 1,800 people at 60 sites across the world, including the Falkland Islands, Ascension Island, Gibraltar, Cyprus and Germany. Of that number, about 1,400 work at the headquarters in Exeter. They have primary functions in research, forecasting and observations, with support for these

from the IT department, which has around 300 staff. IT is a vital function within the Met Office, with the operation of supercomputers for weather forecasting activities. In common with other organizations the Met Office has sales and marketing, business development, human resources, finance, procurement and communications as other functional areas. Within IT, eight professions are recognized, each with a 'guardian of profession'. Of these, the professions of particular relevance here are: ITIL service management, project management, business analysis, people management, and IT architecture and infrastructure.

12.5.2 Where are they now with ITIL, PRINCE2 and DSDM Atern?

The Met Office has used PRINCE2 and ITIL for several years and has only recently begun the implementation of DSDM Atern. The approaches are discussed in the following sections in the sequence in which they were adopted.

12.5.2.1 PRINCE2

PRINCE was introduced in 1998 and the implementation was completed, as a major project, over a four-year period. Before 1998, project management had not been recognized as a separate profession and was integrated with other roles, forming perhaps 25% of an individual's total job. When the implementation began, PROMPT (an earlier version of PRINCE) was being used. Over the years this has been transitioned through PRINCE to PRINCE2 and PRINCE2 (2009).

The implementation was seen as affecting all staff in IT and training was indiscriminate. However, projects were encouraged to adopt the approach and some large and unbeaten projects resulted –

the mammoth project to move the Met Office from Bracknell to Exeter was a PRINCE2 project, phased over the period 2002–2004.

The establishment of PRINCE2 has allowed the Met Office to meet its quality targets and to gain and retain ISO accreditation. PRINCE2 has now been significantly tailored to fit the Met Office needs and ways of working. However, with the introduction of PRINCE2 (2009) the Met Office is moving back to the process in its raw form to capitalize on its best-practice guidance.

12.5.2.2 ITIL

When ITIL first began to be talked about in 2002, a help desk already existed and diverse in-house processes for infrastructure management were in place. The drive came from the IT operations side to develop a more coherent approach to the management of operations and infrastructure.

After initial interest in ITIL in 2002, the adoption of the approach substantially happened over a two-year period between 2007 and 2009. A customer service management group (CSMG) was formed in 2007 to oversee the implementation and operation of ITIL and 10–20 key people were selected to drive the implementation. ITIL process managers were initially appointed for incident, problem and change management. ITIL Foundation training was given widely but Service Manager level training was reserved only for the few who were deemed to really need it.

At the time of writing, the CSMG has now become the strategic marketing and product group. It has a head of service management role and 25 service managers/process owners. Based on identification of this need, a customer experience manager role has been created to represent the customer point of view. The role provides the link between IT support and the business needs.

The Met Office considered applying for ISO 20000 accreditation but decided against this as it did not appear to provide sufficient additional benefit to the organization or fill an identified need. Continual service improvement is embedded and business continuity, alongside IT service continuity is well established. ITIL is still not used for financial management. A decision has been taken to operate this separately.

Future areas of work on ITIL service management include increasing the involvement of service management early in the lifecycle of change projects. Release management involvement already happens early. However, business continuity, availability and capacity management typically do not happen until late in the project lifecycle and it would mitigate certain risks to involve them earlier.

12.5.2.3 DSDM Atern

In 2006, the Met Office identified a need to improve and standardize the software development process within its business change projects. A software tools initiative had highlighted the need for a better process, and an agile way of working was identified as the way forward. An investigation into agile best practice ensued. Met Office project representatives shortlisted three approaches: Scrum, Extreme Programming (XP) and DSDM Atern. Ultimately, Scrum and XP were assessed to be missing sufficient structure in the governance layer and DSDM Atern was selected. 'We tested them all and DSDM Atern was the best.' Training from one of the DSDM Atern accredited training providers began in February 2007 and an intranet-based 'wiki' was built and launched to provide support, guidance and templates for the approach. Many training sessions followed. Training sessions were run for stakeholders from all areas, not just IT, as DSDM Atern is an approach based on teamwork and collaboration between all project disciplines, including the business.

By 2009, DSDM Atern had been used on several projects. It was not fully embedded within Met Office processes and implementations still varied somewhat. In particular, the purpose was sometimes misunderstood and seen as merely 'quick wins' in some quarters. Terminology between DSDM Atern and the other approaches known by staff was often confused to the point where an April Fool's joke email which was sent out with a spoof edict that, 'Because of the proliferation of new terminology, from now on only the following twenty terms will be allowed ...' was widely heralded as an excellent idea! However, timeboxing and MoSCoW techniques were becoming increasingly accepted and providing real benefit, and the wiki was very successful, with projects feeling real ownership of its content, owing to the fact that its users had been encouraged to contribute to it and comment on improvements. A further tranche of training in DSDM Atern is planned into 2010 and beyond to further establish and drive the approach. Its adoption is ongoing.

12.5.3 Order of implementation
PRINCE2, then ITIL and finally DSDM Atern.

12.5.4 Any specific learning points to share with others?
The following key points emerged in answer to this question:

- Don't be too 'precious' about the method itself (whatever method it is). Make it fit your own organization's needs.
- Don't assume because you are using a method, all will be fine!
- Communicate the method to all stakeholders:
  - Project managers
  - Project boards/executives
  - Corporate management
  - Account managers
  - Quality assurance and project assurance
  - Project team members (i.e. developers and testers).
- Benchmark the change of method – capture metrics before the change, to give a comparison.
- Terminology becomes a big, big problem, with each method bringing its own nuances and terms. Create an accepted terms glossary, with translations to the 'old language' and circulate this widely and repeatedly, via training and wikis.
- Allow and enable culture change. Work specifically to change the culture, to see the real benefits of the methods.
- Consider training in methods linked to specific projects – train the team together just before they do the job.
- Ensure projects and change have a clear and prioritized way to start, to avoid the well-meaning 'quick fixes'.
- Do more than one pilot project, and gather metrics.

- Use the PRINCE2 process to implement PRINCE2 – do it as a project!
- Train all stakeholder groups. Ensure PMs get ITIL training (and SMs get PRINCE2 and Atern training).
- Consider the pre-project (pre-PRINCE2 start-up) and post-project needs and responsibilities.
- Identify a clear single SRO for projects/change. Make these sponsors from the business, to make the link to ITIL, service delivery and continuity.
- Keep project boards small (not 50 people!). They are for decision making, not just a communication forum.
- Include a quality management role/person on the project boards.
- Give PRINCE2 projects a 'soft close' to allow for ownership of benefits delivery after the project.
- Start ITIL by getting change management and configuration management right.
- ITIL needs a 'selling' initiative, to show the benefits over the perceived bureaucracy.
- Take account of the whole-life costs of a service. Otherwise, a project may deliver on time and be 'successful' at the expense of delivering huge maintenance and running costs!
- ITIL should not be left to the end of a development project – it doesn't just start with support. The strategy aspects of ITIL should affect/direct the early stages of projects.
- The business case can become too concrete too soon in some projects, and stifles innovation.
- Projects often seen as 'IT projects' and customer perception is that they are IT's responsibility, not theirs and a blame culture can ensue.
- Ensure that training becomes embedded, not just 'lip-service'.
- Training needs to be provided over time for newcomers.
- Accept a standard method, if you can. If the methods are not heavily tailored, it is easier to train newcomers with publicly available training.
- It helps when dealing with supplier and customer companies if a standard best-practice method is known by all parties.

Glossaries

Glossaries

For complete ITIL, and programme, project and risk management glossaries, please visit www.best-management-practice.com/Glossaries-and-Acronyms.

DSDM ATERN GLOSSARY

80:20 rule

A rule of thumb stating that 80% of consequences stem from 20% of causes – for example, 80% of benefits stem from 20% of features. Also known as the Pareto Principle, it advocates pragmatism on a DSDM Atern project.

Atern

Atern is the name given to the latest version of the DSDM framework. It is applicable to all types of change projects, not just software development.

baseline

A snapshot of a product, recorded and preserved at a point in time, as a known status to return to, if necessary.

configuration management (CM)

The discipline of managing the state of a product or set of related products.

deliverable

A product. Something produced during the project.

deployment

A lifecycle phase that focuses on getting the solution or part of it into operational use.

development timebox

The lowest level of timebox. It is this timebox that would be divided into cycles of investigation, refinement and consolidation.

DSDM/DSDM Consortium

The DSDM Consortium is the guardian of the DSDM Atern framework. DSDM stands for Dynamic Systems Development Method.

engineering

A lifecycle phase used iteratively and incrementally to evolve the solution created during exploration to operational readiness.

exploration

A lifecycle phase used iteratively and incrementally to investigate the requirements in detail and translate them into a form which can then be evolved into a viable solution.

facilitated workshop

A facilitated workshop is a gathering together of a group of people with the right skills and empowerment to produce a required product. It is coordinated by an impartial facilitator, who enables the group to work collaboratively to achieve a predetermined objective.

facilitator

An independent role in a workshop, responsible for the workshop process and managing the group dynamics.

feasibility

A lifecycle phase that gives the first opportunity for deciding whether or not the project is viable from a technical and business perspective.

foundations

A lifecycle phase to establish a firm basis for the rest of the project, from the three perspectives (domains) of business, solutions and management.

framework

A collection of principles, processes, roles and practices that provide a way to run projects. Framework is a similar term to 'method' and 'approach'.

functional requirement

A definition of an aspect of WHAT the product of the project needs to do to satisfy business need and the project objective. A feature or function. A user story.

increment

A partial delivery of the final product, preferably into operational use if possible. The term can also be used to describe a part of the project which creates a delivery of product.

issue

Any concern, query or event that has happened, or is happening, that affects the project.

iterative development

A DSDM Atern technique that allows evolution of a solution by prototyping and successive passes through investigation, refinement and consolidation. It allows validation of the understanding of the business needs and verification that the solution is being built correctly. It is used as a technique for communication and prototyping to converge on an accurate solution.

lifecycle

A series of phases a project goes through. The DSDM Atern Lifecycle has seven phases.

minimum usable subset

The minimum amount of a project that needs to be delivered in order to provide a workable solution. The 'must haves'.

model

A representation of some or all of a product, produced in order to aid understanding or facilitate testing. It is usually a diagram, a picture or a prototype.

MoSCoW

A prioritization technique used on requirements and tests, where M stands for must have, S stands for should have, C stands for could have and W stands for won't have this time.

non-functional requirement

A performance attribute. This can relate to the products of a project, a requirement, or a group of requirements. It specifies 'how well' or 'to what level' the product needs to perform. Examples of non-functional requirements are: performance, response time, security, availability, reliability.

phase

A part of the DSDM Atern lifecycle. There are seven phases in the DSDM Atern lifecycle.

post-project

The DSDM Atern lifecycle phase which takes place after the last deployment, where benefits realization is assessed.

pre-project

The DSDM Atern lifecycle phase where the initial idea or imperative for a project is formalized in order for a project to be initiated.

principle

A 'natural law' which acts as an attitude to take and a mindset to adopt on a DSDM Atern project.

prioritized requirements list (PRL)

A list of requirements for the project, which have been prioritized using the MoSCoW technique.

product

The name given to deliverables produced during the DSDM Atern lifecycle. A product could be a document, a prototype, an interim solution or the final outcome of a project.

product description

A description of the structure of a product, which provides guidance on what the product should contain, its quality criteria and reviewers.

project approach questionnaire (PAQ)

A series of questions designed to establish a favourable environment for the conduct of a DSDM Atern project, where the eight principles can be adhered to and risks to project success are minimized.

prototype

A disposable or evolutionary piece of work to demonstrate how an objective has been, or can be achieved. An exploratory version of part of the final solution. The evolution of prototypes through iterative development is fundamental to DSDM Atern.

requirement

A stated business need. A 'function' or 'feature'. Something that the final solution needs to do or exhibit.

responsibilities

Specific tasks and duties associated with a role.

retrospective

A facilitated workshop to look back at the work done over a period, often a timebox, to assess what went well and what can be learned.

risk

An event which may have an effect on the project. This can be negative or positive.

role

A set of responsibilities allocated to an individual or individuals within a DSDM project.

scope

A description of the aspects of the business or organization which the project is intended to cover. This could be a list of features and/or a description of areas which may be included in the project (or which may be specifically excluded).

technique

A part of the DSDM Atern method which is used to help with the execution of a project. There are five techniques in DSDM Atern. These are timeboxing, MoSCoW, facilitated workshops, modelling and iterative development (also referred to as 'prototyping').

timebox

A period of time, at the end of which a business objective will be met and a completed product produced. There are different types of timebox operating at different levels. These are: Project Timebox, Increment Timebox and Development Timebox.

velocity

The speed at which the solution development team is working. This may be expressed in terms of numbers of features or story points completed in a timebox. Metrics related to this across many timeboxes can help a team to establish a sustainable pace of working.

ITIL GLOSSARY

The core publication names (*Service Strategy, Service Design, Service Operation, Service Transition, Continual Service Improvement*) included in parentheses after the name of a term indicate where a reader can find more information. Terms without an accompanying reference may be used generally in all five core publications, or may not be defined in any greater detail elsewhere. In other words, readers are only directed to other sources where they can expect to expand on their knowledge or to see a greater context.

access management

(*Service Operation*) The process responsible for allowing users to make use of IT services, data or other assets. Access management helps to protect the confidentiality, integrity and availability of assets by ensuring that only authorized users are able to access or modify the assets. Access management is sometimes referred to as rights management or identity management.

account manager

(*Service Strategy*) A role that is very similar to that of the business relationship manager, but includes more commercial aspects. Most commonly used when dealing with external customers.

accounting

(*Service Strategy*) The process responsible for identifying the actual costs of delivering IT services, comparing these with budgeted costs, and managing variance from the budget.

activity

A set of actions designed to achieve a particular result. Activities are usually defined as part of processes or plans, and are documented in procedures.

application management

(*Service Design*) (*Service Operation*) The function responsible for managing applications throughout their lifecycle.

architecture

(*Service Design*) The structure of a system or IT service, including the relationships of components to each other and to the environment they are in. Architecture also includes the standards and guidelines that guide the design and evolution of the system.

asset

(*Service Strategy*) Any resource or capability. The assets of a service provider include anything that could contribute to the delivery of a service. Assets can be one of the following types: management, organization, process, knowledge, people, information, applications, infrastructure, financial capital.

audit

Formal inspection and verification to check whether a standard or set of guidelines is being followed, that records are accurate, or that efficiency and effectiveness targets are being met. An audit may be carried out by internal or external groups. *See also* assessment; certification.

availability

(*Service Design*) Ability of an IT service or other configuration item to perform its agreed function when required. Availability is determined by reliability, maintainability, serviceability, performance and security. Availability is usually calculated as a percentage. This calculation is often based on agreed service time and downtime. It is best practice to calculate availability of an IT service using measurements of the business output.

availability management

(*Service Design*) The process responsible for defining, analysing, planning, measuring and improving all aspects of the availability of IT services. Availability management is responsible for ensuring that all IT infrastructure, processes, tools, roles etc. are appropriate for the agreed service level targets for availability.

budgeting

The activity of predicting and controlling the spending of money. Budgeting consists of a periodic negotiation cycle to set future budgets (usually annual) and the day-to-day monitoring and adjusting of current budgets.

build

(*Service Transition*) The activity of assembling a number of configuration items to create part of an IT service. The term is also used to refer to a release that is authorized for distribution – for example, server build or laptop build.

business

(*Service Strategy*) An overall corporate entity or organization formed of a number of business units. In the context of ITSM, the term includes public sector and not-for-profit organizations, as well as companies. An IT service provider provides IT services to a customer within a business. The IT service provider may be part of the same business as its customer (internal service provider), or part of another business (external service provider).

business case

(*Service Strategy*) Justification for a significant item of expenditure. The business case includes information about costs, benefits, options, issues, risks and possible problems.

business continuity management

(*Service Design*) The business process responsible for managing risks that could seriously affect the business. Business continuity management safeguards the interests of key stakeholders, reputation, brand and value-creating activities. The process involves reducing risks to an acceptable level and planning for the recovery of business processes should a disruption to the business occur. Business continuity management sets the objectives, scope and requirements for IT service continuity management.

business continuity plan

(*Service Design*) A plan defining the steps required to restore business processes following a disruption. The plan will also identify the triggers for invocation, people to be involved, communications etc. IT service continuity plans form a significant part of business continuity plans.

business objective

(*Service Strategy*) The objective of a business process, or of the business as a whole. Business objectives support the business vision, provide guidance for the IT strategy, and are often supported by IT services.

business perspective

(*Continual Service Improvement*) An understanding of the service provider and IT services from the point of view of the business, and an understanding of the business from the point of view of the service provider.

business process

A process that is owned and carried out by the business. A business process contributes to the delivery of a product or service to a business customer. For example, a retailer may have a purchasing process that helps to deliver services to its business customers. Many business processes rely on IT services.

capability

(*Service Strategy*) The ability of an organization, person, process, application, IT service or other configuration item to carry out an activity. Capabilities are intangible assets of an organization. *See also* resource.

capacity management

(*Service Design*) The process responsible for ensuring that the capacity of IT services and the IT infrastructure is able to deliver agreed service level targets in a cost-effective and timely manner. Capacity management considers all resources required to deliver the IT service, and plans for short-, medium- and long-term business requirements.

capacity plan

(*Service Design*) A capacity plan is used to manage the resources required to deliver IT services. The plan contains scenarios for different predictions of business demand, and costed options to deliver the agreed service level targets.

Change Advisory Board

(*Service Transition*) A group of people who advise the change manager in the assessment, prioritization and scheduling of changes. This board is usually made up of representatives from all areas within the IT service provider, representatives from the business, and third parties such as suppliers.

change management

(*Service Transition*) The process responsible for controlling the lifecycle of all changes. The primary objective of change management is to enable beneficial changes to be made, with minimum disruption to IT services.

charging

(*Service Strategy*) Requiring payment for IT services. Charging for IT services is optional, and many organizations choose to treat their IT service provider as a cost centre.

closed

(*Service Operation*) The final status in the lifecycle of an incident, problem, change etc. When the status is closed, no further action is taken.

compliance

Ensuring that a standard or set of guidelines is followed, or that proper, consistent accounting or other practices are being employed.

configuration item

(*Service Transition*) Any component that needs to be managed in order to deliver an IT service. Information about each configuration item is recorded in a configuration record within the configuration management system and is maintained throughout its lifecycle by configuration management. Configuration items are under the control of change management. They typically include IT services, hardware, software, buildings, people and formal documentation such as process documentation and service level agreements.

configuration management

(*Service Transition*) The process responsible for maintaining information about configuration items required to deliver an IT service, including their relationships. This information is managed throughout the lifecycle of the configuration item. Configuration management is part of an overall service asset and configuration management process.

configuration management system

(*Service Transition*) A set of tools and databases that are used to manage an IT service provider's configuration data. The configuration management system also includes information about incidents, problems, known errors, changes and releases, and may contain data about employees, suppliers, locations, business units, customers and users. The configuration management system includes tools for collecting, storing, managing, updating and presenting data about all configuration items and their relationships. The configuration management system is maintained by configuration management and is used by all IT service management processes. *See also* service knowledge management system.

continual service improvement

(*Continual Service Improvement*) A stage in the lifecycle of an IT service and the title of one of the core ITIL publications. Continual service improvement is responsible for managing improvements to IT service management processes and IT services. The performance of the IT service provider is continually measured and improvements are made to processes, IT services and IT infrastructure in order to increase efficiency, effectiveness and cost-effectiveness.

contract

A legally binding agreement between two or more parties.

cost

The amount of money spent on a specific activity, IT service or business unit. Costs consist of real cost (money), notional cost (such as people's time) and depreciation.

culture

A set of values that is shared by a group of people, including expectations about how people should behave, their ideas, beliefs and practices.

customer

Someone who buys goods or services. The customer of an IT service provider is the person or group who defines and agrees the service level targets. The term is also sometimes informally used to mean user – for example, 'This is a customer-focused organization.'

deliverable

Something that must be provided to meet a commitment in a service level agreement or a contract. It is also used in a more informal way to mean a planned output of any process.

demand management

Activities that understand and influence customer demand for services and the provision of capacity to meet these demands. At a strategic level, demand management can involve analysis of patterns of business activity and user profiles. At a tactical level, it can involve use of differential charging to encourage customers to use IT services at less busy times. *See also* capacity management.

deployment

(*Service Transition*) The activity responsible for movement of new or changed hardware, software, documentation, process etc. to the live environment. Deployment is part of the release and deployment management process.

design

(*Service Design*) An activity or process that identifies requirements and then defines a solution that is able to meet these requirements. *See also* service design.

development

(*Service Design*) The process responsible for creating or modifying an IT service or application. Also used to mean the role or group that carries out development work.

development environment

(*Service Design*) An environment used to create or modify IT services or applications. Development environments are not typically subjected to the same degree of control as test or live environments. *See also* development.

downtime

(*Service Design*) (*Service Operation*) The time when an IT service or other configuration item is not available during its agreed service time. The availability of an IT service is often calculated from agreed service time and downtime.

early life support

(*Service Transition*) Support provided for a new or changed IT service for a period of time after it is released. During early life support, the IT service provider may review the key performance indicators, service levels and monitoring thresholds, and provide additional resources for incident and problem management.

Emergency Change Advisory Board

(*Service Transition*) A subgroup of the Change Advisory Board that makes decisions about high-impact emergency changes. Membership may be decided at the time a meeting is called, and depends on the nature of the emergency change.

environment

(*Service Transition*) A subset of the IT infrastructure that is used for a particular purpose – for example, live environment, test environment, build environment. Also used in the term 'physical environment' to mean the accommodation, air conditioning, power system etc. Environment is used as a generic term to mean the external conditions that influence or affect something.

escalation

(*Service Operation*) An activity that obtains additional resources when these are needed to meet service level targets or customer expectations. Escalation may be needed within any IT service management process, but is most commonly associated with incident management, problem management and the management of customer complaints. There are two types of escalation: functional escalation and hierarchic escalation.

evaluation

(*Service Transition*) The process responsible for assessing a new or changed IT service to ensure that risks have been managed and to help determine whether to proceed with the change. Evaluation is also used to mean comparing an actual outcome with the intended outcome, or comparing one alternative with another.

event

(*Service Operation*) A change of state that has significance for the management of an IT service or other configuration item. The term is also used to mean an alert or notification created by any IT service, configuration item or monitoring tool. Events typically require IT operations personnel to take actions, and often lead to incidents being logged.

external customer

A customer who works for a different business from the IT service provider.

facilities management

(*Service Operation*) The function responsible for managing the physical environment where the IT infrastructure is located. Facilities management includes all aspects of managing the physical environment – for example, power and cooling, building access management, and environmental monitoring.

financial management

(*Service Strategy*) The function and processes responsible for managing an IT service provider's budgeting, accounting and charging requirements.

fit for purpose

An informal term used to describe a process, configuration item, IT service etc. that is capable of meeting its objectives or service levels. Being fit for purpose requires suitable design, implementation, control and maintenance.

function

A team or group of people and the tools they use to carry out one or more processes or activities – for example, the service desk. The term also has two other meanings:

● An intended purpose of a configuration item, person, team, process or IT service. For example, one function of an e-mail service may be to store and forward outgoing mails, while the function of a business process may be to despatch goods to customers.

● To perform the intended purpose correctly, as in 'The computer is functioning.'

gap analysis

(*Continual Service Improvement*) An activity that compares two sets of data and identifies the differences. Gap analysis is commonly used to compare a set of requirements with actual delivery.

governance

Ensuring that policies and strategy are actually implemented, and that required processes are correctly followed. Governance includes defining roles and responsibilities, measuring and reporting, and taking actions to resolve any issues identified.

impact

(*Service Operation*) (*Service Transition*) A measure of the effect of an incident, problem or change on business processes. Impact is often based on how service levels will be affected. Impact and urgency are used to assign priority.

incident

(*Service Operation*) An unplanned interruption to an IT service or reduction in the quality of an IT service. Failure of a configuration item that has not yet affected service is also an incident – for example, failure of one disk from a mirror set.

incident management

(*Service Operation*) The process responsible for managing the lifecycle of all incidents. The primary objective of incident management is to return the IT service to customers as quickly as possible.

information security management

(*Service Design*) The process that ensures the confidentiality, integrity and availability of an organization's assets, information, data and IT services. Information security management usually forms part of an organizational approach to security management that has a wider scope than the IT service provider, and includes handling of paper, building access, phone calls etc. for the entire organization.

information technology

The use of technology for the storage, communication or processing of information. The technology typically includes computers, telecommunications, applications and other software. The information may include business data, voice, images, video etc. Information technology is often used to support business processes through IT services.

International Organization for Standardization

The International Organization for Standardization (ISO) is the world's largest developer of standards. ISO is a non-governmental organization that is a network of the national standards institutes of 156 countries. See www.iso.org for further information about ISO.

ISO/IEC 20000

ISO specification and code of practice for IT service management. ISO/IEC 20000 is aligned with ITIL best practice.

ISO/IEC 27001

(*Continual Service Improvement*) (*Service Design*) ISO specification for information security management. The corresponding code of practice is ISO/IEC 17799.

IT infrastructure

All of the hardware, software, networks, facilities etc. that are required to develop, test, deliver, monitor, control or support IT services. The term includes all of the information technology but not the associated people, processes and documentation.

IT infrastructure library

A set of best-practice guidance for IT service management. ITIL is owned by the OGC and consists of a series of publications giving guidance on the provision of quality IT services, and on the processes and facilities needed to support them. See www.itil.co.uk for more information.

IT service

A service provided to one or more customers by an IT service provider. An IT service is based on the use of information technology and supports the customer's business processes. It is made up of a combination of people, processes and technology and should be defined in a service level agreement.

IT service continuity management

(*Service Design*) The process responsible for managing risks that could seriously affect IT services. IT service continuity management ensures that the IT service provider can always provide minimum agreed service levels, by reducing the risk to an acceptable level and planning for the recovery of IT services. IT service continuity management should be designed to support business continuity management.

IT service management

The implementation and management of quality IT services that meet the needs of the business. IT service management is performed by IT service providers through an appropriate mix of people, processes and information technology. *See also* service management.

IT Steering Group

A formal group that is responsible for ensuring that business and IT service provider strategies and plans are closely aligned. An IT Steering Group includes senior representatives from the business and the IT service provider.

knowledge management

(*Service Transition*) The process responsible for gathering, analysing, storing and sharing knowledge and information within an organization. The primary purpose of knowledge management is to improve efficiency by reducing the need to rediscover knowledge. *See also* service knowledge management system.

known error database

(*Service Operation*) A database containing all known error records. This database is created by problem management and used by incident and problem management. The known error database is part of the configuration management system.

lifecycle

The various stages in the life of an IT service, configuration item, incident, problem, change etc. The lifecycle defines the categories for status and the status transitions that are permitted. For example:

- The lifecycle of an application includes requirements, design, build, deploy, operate, optimize

- The expanded incident lifecycle includes detect, respond, diagnose, repair, recover, restore

- The lifecycle of a server may include: ordered, received, in test, live, disposed etc.

live environment

(*Service Transition*) A controlled environment containing live configuration items used to deliver IT services to customers.

maintainability

(*Service Design*) A measure of how quickly and effectively an IT service or other configuration item can be restored to normal working after a failure. Maintainability is often measured and reported as MTRS. Maintainability is also used in the context of software or IT service development to mean ability to be changed or repaired easily.

metric

(*Continual Service Improvement*) Something that is measured and reported to help manage a process, IT service or activity.

model

A representation of a system, process, IT service, configuration item etc. that is used to help understand or predict future behaviour.

monitoring

(*Service Operation*) Repeated observation of a configuration item, IT service or process to detect events and to ensure that the current status is known.

objective

The defined purpose or aim of a process, an activity or an organization as a whole. Objectives are usually expressed as measurable targets. The term is also informally used to mean a requirement.

Office of Government Commerce

OGC owns the ITIL brand (copyright and trademark). OGC is a UK government department that supports the delivery of the government's procurement agenda through its work in collaborative procurement and in raising levels of procurement skills and capability within departments. It also provides support for complex public sector projects.

operational level agreement

(*Continual Service Improvement*) (*Service Design*) An agreement between an IT service provider and another part of the same organization. It supports the IT service provider's delivery of IT services to customers and defines the goods or services to be provided and the responsibilities of both parties. For example, there could be an operational level agreement:

- Between the IT service provider and a procurement department to obtain hardware in agreed times

- Between the service desk and a support group to provide incident resolution in agreed times.

See also service level agreement.

organization

A company, legal entity or other institution. Examples of organizations that are not companies include the International Standards Organization and itSMF. The term is sometimes used to refer to any entity that has people, resources and budgets – for example, a project or business unit.

pilot

(*Service Transition*) A limited deployment of an IT service, a release or a process to the live environment. A pilot is used to reduce risk and to gain user feedback and acceptance. *See also* test.

plan

A detailed proposal that describes the activities and resources needed to achieve an objective – for example, a plan to implement a new IT service or process. ISO/IEC 20000 requires a plan for the management of each IT service management process.

post-implementation review

A review that takes place after a change or a project has been implemented. It determines if the change or project was successful, and identifies opportunities for improvement.

PRINCE2

The standard UK government methodology for project management. See www.ogc.gov.uk/prince2 for more information.

priority

(*Service Operation*) (*Service Transition*) A category used to identify the relative importance of an incident, problem or change. Priority is based on impact and urgency, and is used to identify required times for actions to be taken. For example, the service level agreement may state that Priority 2 incidents must be resolved within 12 hours.

problem

(*Service Operation*) A cause of one or more incidents. The cause is not usually known at the time a problem record is created, and the problem management process is responsible for further investigation.

problem management

(*Service Operation*) The process responsible for managing the lifecycle of all problems. The primary objectives of problem management are to prevent incidents from happening, and to minimize the impact of incidents that cannot be prevented.

procedure

A document containing steps that specify how to achieve an activity. Procedures are defined as part of processes.

process

A structured set of activities designed to accomplish a specific objective. A process takes one or more defined inputs and turns them into defined outputs. It may include any of the roles, responsibilities, tools and management controls required to reliably deliver the outputs. A process may define policies, standards, guidelines, activities and work instructions if they are needed.

process manager

A role responsible for the operational management of a process. The process manager's responsibilities include planning and coordination of all activities required to carry out, monitor and report on the process. There may be several process managers for one process – for example, regional change managers or IT service continuity managers for each data centre. The process manager role is often assigned to the person who carries out the process owner role, but the two roles may be separate in larger organizations.

process owner

A role responsible for ensuring that a process is fit for purpose. The process owner's responsibilities include sponsorship, design, change management and continual improvement of the process and its metrics. This role is often assigned to the same person who carries out the process manager role, but the two roles may be separate in larger organizations.

product manager

(*Service Strategy*) A role responsible for managing one or more services throughout their entire lifecycle. Product managers are instrumental in the development of service strategy and are responsible for the content of the service portfolio.

programme

A number of projects and activities that are planned and managed together to achieve an overall set of related objectives and other outcomes.

project

A temporary organization, with people and other assets, that is required to achieve an objective or other outcome. Each project has a lifecycle that typically includes initiation, planning, execution, closure etc. Projects are usually managed using a formal methodology such as PRINCE2.

quality

The ability of a product, service or process to provide the intended value. For example, a hardware component can be considered to be of high quality if it performs as expected and delivers the required reliability. Process quality also requires an ability to monitor effectiveness and efficiency, and to improve them if necessary.

quality assurance

(*Service Transition*) The process responsible for ensuring that the quality of a product, service or process will provide its intended value.

recovery

(*Service Design*) (*Service Operation*) Returning a configuration item or an IT service to a working state. Recovery of an IT service often includes recovering data to a known consistent state. After recovery, further steps may be needed before the IT service can be made available to the users (restoration).

release

(*Service Transition*) A collection of hardware, software, documentation, processes or other components required to implement one or more approved changes to IT services. The contents of each release are managed, tested and deployed as a single entity.

release management

(*Service Transition*) The process responsible for planning, scheduling and controlling the movement of releases to test and live environments. The primary objective of release management is to ensure that the integrity of the live environment is protected and that the correct components are released. Release management is part of the release and deployment management process.

reliability

(*Continual Service Improvement*) (*Service Design*) A measure of how long an IT service or other configuration item can perform its agreed function without interruption. Usually measured as MTBF or MTBSI. The term can also be used to state how likely it is that a process, function etc. will deliver its required outputs.

request for change

(*Service Transition*) A formal proposal for a change to be made. It includes details of the proposed change, and may be recorded on paper or electronically. The term is often misused to mean a change record, or the change itself.

requirement

(*Service Design*) A formal statement of what is needed – for example, a service level requirement, a project requirement or the required deliverables for a process. *See also* statement of requirements.

resource

(*Service Strategy*) A generic term that includes IT infrastructure, people, money or anything else that might help to deliver an IT service. Resources are considered to be assets of an organization. *See also* service asset.

return on investment

(*Continual Service Improvement*) (*Service Strategy*) A measurement of the expected benefit of an investment. In the simplest sense, it is the net profit of an investment divided by the net worth of the assets invested.

review

An evaluation of a change, problem, process, project etc. Reviews are typically carried out at predefined points in the lifecycle, and especially after closure. The purpose of a review is to ensure that all deliverables have been provided, and to identify opportunities for improvement. *See also* post-implementation review.

risk

A possible event that could cause harm or loss, or affect the ability to achieve objectives. A risk is measured by the probability of a threat, the vulnerability of the asset to that threat, and the impact it would have if it occurred.

risk management

The process responsible for identifying, assessing and controlling risks.

role

A set of responsibilities, activities and authorities granted to a person or team. A role is defined in a process. One person or team may have multiple roles – for example, the roles of configuration manager and change manager may be carried out by a single person.

root cause

(*Service Operation*) The underlying or original cause of an incident or problem.

scope

The boundary or extent to which a process, procedure, certification, contract etc. applies. For example, the scope of change management may include all live IT services and related configuration items; the scope of an ISO/IEC 20000 certificate may include all IT services delivered out of a named data centre.

server

(*Service Operation*) A computer that is connected to a network and provides software functions that are used by other computers.

service

A means of delivering value to customers by facilitating outcomes customers want to achieve without the ownership of specific costs and risks. *See also* IT service.

service asset

Any capability or resource of a service provider.

service asset and configuration management

(*Service Transition*) The process responsible for both configuration management and asset management.

service catalogue

(*Service Design*) A database or structured document with information about all live IT services, including those available for deployment. The service catalogue is the only part of the service portfolio published to customers, and is used to support the sale and delivery of IT services. The service catalogue includes information about deliverables, prices, contact points, ordering and request processes.

service design

(*Service Design*) A stage in the lifecycle of an IT service. Service design includes a number of processes and functions and is the title of one of the core ITIL publications.

service design package

(*Service Design*) Document(s) defining all aspects of an IT service and its requirements through each stage of its lifecycle. A service design package is produced for each new IT service, major change or IT service retirement.

service desk

(*Service Operation*) The single point of contact between the service provider and the users. A typical service desk manages incidents and service requests, and also handles communication with the users.

service knowledge management system

(*Service Transition*) A set of tools and databases that are used to manage knowledge and information. The service knowledge management system includes the configuration management system, as well as other tools and databases. It stores, manages, updates and presents all information that an IT service provider needs to manage the full lifecycle of IT services.

service level agreement

(*Continual Service Improvement*) (*Service Design*) An agreement between an IT service provider and a customer. A service level agreement describes the IT service, documents service level targets, and specifies the responsibilities of the IT service provider and the customer. A single agreement may cover multiple IT services or multiple customers. *See also* operational level agreement.

service level package

(*Service Strategy*) A defined level of utility and warranty for a particular service package. Each service level package is designed to meet the needs of a particular pattern of business activity.

service level requirement

(*Continual Service Improvement*) (*Service Design*) A customer requirement for an aspect of an IT service. Service level requirements are based on business objectives and used to negotiate agreed service level targets.

service management

Service management is a set of specialized organizational capabilities for providing value to customers in the form of services.

service management lifecycle

An approach to IT service management that emphasizes the importance of coordination and control across the various functions, processes and systems necessary to manage the full lifecycle of IT services. The service management lifecycle approach considers the strategy, design, transition, operation and continuous improvement of IT services. Also known as service lifecycle.

service manager

A manager who is responsible for managing the end-to-end lifecycle of one or more IT services. The term is also used to mean any manager within the IT service provider. Most commonly used to refer to a business relationship manager, a process manager, an account manager or a senior manager with responsibility for IT services overall.

service operation

(*Service Operation*) A stage in the lifecycle of an IT service. Service operation includes a number of processes and functions and is the title of one of the core ITIL publications.

service owner

(*Continual Service Improvement*) A role that is accountable for the delivery of a specific IT service.

service pipeline

(*Service Strategy*) A database or structured document listing all IT services that are under consideration or development, but are not yet available to customers. The service pipeline provides a business view of possible future IT services and is part of the service portfolio that is not normally published to customers.

service portfolio

(*Service Strategy*) The complete set of services that are managed by a service provider. The service portfolio is used to manage the entire lifecycle of all services, and includes three categories: service pipeline (proposed or in development), service catalogue (live or available for deployment) and retired services.

service provider

(*Service Strategy*) An organization supplying services to one or more internal customers or external customers. Service provider is often used as an abbreviation for IT service provider. *See also* Type I service provider; Type II service provider; Type III service provider.

service request

(*Service Operation*) A request from a user for information or advice, for a standard change or for access to an IT service – for example, to reset a password or to provide standard IT services for a new user. Service requests are usually handled by a service desk and do not require a request for change to be submitted.

service strategy

(*Service Strategy*) The title of one of the core ITIL publications. Service strategy establishes an overall strategy for IT services and for IT service management.

service transition

(*Service Transition*) A stage in the lifecycle of an IT service. Service transition includes a number of processes and functions and is the title of one of the core ITIL publications.

service validation and testing

(*Service Transition*) The process responsible for validation and testing of a new or changed IT service. Service validation and testing ensures that the IT service matches its design specification and will meet the needs of the business.

single point of contact

(*Service Operation*) Providing a single consistent way to communicate with an organization or business unit. For example, a single point of contact for an IT service provider is usually called a service desk.

specification

A formal definition of requirements. A specification may be used to define technical or operational requirements, and may be internal or external. Many public standards consist of a code of practice and a specification. The specification defines the standard against which an organization can be audited.

stakeholder

All people who have an interest in an organization, project, IT service etc. Stakeholders may be interested in the activities, targets, resources or deliverables. Stakeholders may include customers, partners, employees, shareholders, owners etc.

statement of requirements

(*Service Design*) A document containing all requirements for a product purchase, or a new or changed IT service. *See also* terms of reference.

super user

(*Service Operation*) A user who helps other users, and assists in communication with the service desk or other parts of the IT service provider. Super users typically provide support for minor incidents and training.

supplier

(*Service Design*) (*Service Strategy*) A third party responsible for supplying goods or services that are required to deliver IT services. Examples of suppliers include commodity hardware and software vendors, network and telecom providers, and outsourcing organizations. *See also* underpinning contract.

supplier management

(*Service Design*) The process responsible for ensuring that all contracts with suppliers support the needs of the business, and that all suppliers meet their contractual commitments.

system

A number of related things that work together to achieve an overall objective. For example:

- A computer system including hardware, software and applications

- A management system, including multiple processes that are planned and managed together – for example, a quality management system

- A database management system or operating system that includes many software modules that are designed to perform a set of related functions.

terms of reference

(*Service Design*) A document specifying the requirements, scope, deliverables, resources and schedule for a project or activity.

test

(*Service Transition*) An activity that verifies that a configuration item, IT service, process etc. meets its specification or agreed requirements. *See also* service validation and testing.

third party

A person, group or business that is not part of the service level agreement for an IT service, but is required to ensure successful delivery of that IT service – for example, a software supplier, a hardware maintenance company or a facilities department. Requirements for third parties are typically specified in underpinning contracts or operational level agreements.

threat

A threat is anything that might exploit a vulnerability. Any potential cause of an incident can be considered a threat. For example, a fire is a threat that could exploit the vulnerability of flammable floor coverings. This term is commonly used in information security management and IT service continuity management, but also applies to other areas such as problem and availability management.

total cost of ownership

(*Service Strategy*) A methodology used to help make investment decisions. It assesses the full lifecycle cost of owning a configuration item, not just the initial cost or purchase price.

transition planning and support

(*Service Transition*) The process responsible for planning all service transition processes and coordinating the resources that they require. These service transition processes are change management, service asset and configuration management, release and deployment management, service validation and testing, evaluation, and knowledge management.

Type I service provider

(*Service Strategy*) An internal service provider that is embedded within a business unit. There may be several Type I service providers within an organization.

Type II service provider

(*Service Strategy*) An internal service provider that provides shared IT services to more than one business unit.

Type III service provider

(*Service Strategy*) A service provider that provides IT services to external customers.

underpinning contract

(*Service Design*) A contract between an IT service provider and a third party. The third party provides goods or services that support delivery of an IT service to a customer. The underpinning contract defines targets and responsibilities that are required to meet agreed service level targets in a service level agreement.

user

A person who uses the IT service on a day-to-day basis. Users are distinct from customers, as some customers do not use the IT service directly.

utility

(*Service Strategy*) Functionality offered by a product or service to meet a particular need. Utility is often summarized as 'what it does', and may be used as a synonym for service utility.

verification

(*Service Transition*) An activity that ensures that a new or changed IT service, process, plan or other deliverable is complete, accurate, reliable and matches its design specification. See *also* acceptance; service validation and testing.

version

(*Service Transition*) A version is used to identify a specific baseline of a configuration item. Versions typically use a naming convention that enables the sequence or date of each baseline to be identified. For example, payroll application version 3 contains updated functionality from version 2.

warranty

(*Service Strategy*) A promise or guarantee that a product or service will meet its agreed requirements. Warranty is often used as a synonym for service warranty. *See also* service validation and testing.

PRINCE2 GLOSSARY

acceptance criteria

A prioritized list of criteria that the project product must meet before the customer will accept it, i.e. measurable definitions of the attributes required for the set of products to be acceptable to key stakeholders.

activity

A process, function or task that occurs over time, has recognizable results and is managed. It is usually defined as part of a process or plan.

agile methods

Principally, software development methods that apply the project approach of using short time-boxed iterations where products are incrementally developed. PRINCE2 is compatible with agile principles.

baseline

Reference levels against which an entity is monitored and controlled.

benefit

The measurable improvement resulting from an outcome perceived as an advantage by one or more stakeholders.

benefits review plan

A plan that defines how and when a measurement of the achievement of the project's benefits can be made. If the project is being managed within a programme, this information may be created and maintained at the programme level.

business case

The justification for an organizational activity (project), which typically contains costs, benefits, risks and timescales, and against which continuing viability is tested.

change authority

A person or group to which the project board may delegate responsibility for the consideration of requests for change or off-specifications. The change authority may be given a change budget and can approve changes within that budget.

change control

The procedure that ensures that all changes that may affect the project's agreed objectives are identified, assessed and either approved, rejected or deferred.

communication management strategy

A description of the means and frequency of communication between the project and the project's stakeholders.

configuration item

An entity that is subject to configuration management. The entity may be a component of a product, a product, or a set of products in a release.

configuration management

Technical and administrative activities concerned with the creation, maintenance and controlled change of configuration throughout the life of a product.

configuration management strategy

A description of how and by whom the project's products will be controlled and protected.

configuration management system

The set of processes, tools and databases that are used to manage configuration data. Typically, a project will use the configuration management system of either the customer or supplier organization.

customer

The person or group who commissioned the work and will benefit from the end results.

DSDM Atern

An agile project delivery framework developed and owned by the DSDM consortium. Atern uses a timeboxed and iterative approach to product development and is compatible with PRINCE2.

embedding (PRINCE2)

What an organization needs to do to adopt PRINCE2 as its corporate project management method. See also, in contrast, 'tailoring', which defines what a project needs to do to apply the method to a specific project environment.

exception

A situation where it can be forecast that there will be a deviation beyond the tolerance levels agreed between project manager and project board (or between project board and corporate or programme management).

executive

The single individual with overall responsibility for ensuring that a project meets its objectives and delivers the projected benefits. This individual should ensure that the project maintains its business focus, that it has clear authority, and that the work, including risks, is actively managed. The executive is the chair of the project board. He or she represents the customer and is responsible for the business case.

governance (corporate)

The ongoing activity of maintaining a sound system of internal control by which the directors and officers of an organization ensure that effective management systems, including financial monitoring and control systems, have been put in place to protect assets, earning capacity and the reputation of the organization.

governance (project)

Those areas of corporate governance that are specifically related to project activities. Effective governance of project management ensures that an organization's project portfolio is aligned to the organization's objectives, is delivered efficiently and is sustainable.

handover

The transfer of ownership of a set of products to the respective user(s). The set of products is known as a release. There may be more than one handover in the life of a project (phased delivery). The final handover takes place in the Closing a Project process.

issue

A relevant event that has happened, was not planned, and requires management action. It can be any concern, query, request for change, suggestion or off-specification raised during a project. Project issues can be about anything to do with the project.

issue register

A register used to capture and maintain information on all of the issues that are being managed formally. The issue register should be monitored by the project manager on a regular basis.

lessons log

An informal repository for lessons that apply to this project or future projects.

management product

A product that will be required as part of managing the project, and establishing and maintaining quality (for example, highlight report, end stage report etc.). The management products stay constant, whatever the type of project, and can be used as described, or with any relevant modifications, for all projects. There are three types of management product: baselines, records and reports.

management stage

The section of a project that the project manager is managing on behalf of the project board at any one time, at the end of which the project board will wish to review progress to date, the state of the project plan, the business case and risks, and the next stage plan in order to decide whether to continue with the project.

off-specification

Something that should be provided by the project, but currently is not (or is forecast not to be) provided. This might be a missing product or a product not meeting its specifications. It is one type of issue.

output

A specialist product that is handed over to a user(s). Note that management products are not outputs but are created solely for the purpose of managing the project.

plan

A detailed proposal for doing or achieving something which specifies the what, when, how and by whom. In PRINCE2 there are only the following types of plan: project plan, stage plan, team plan, exception plan and benefits review plan.

premature closure

The PRINCE2 activity to close a project before its planned closure. The project manager must ensure that work in progress is not simply abandoned, but that the project salvages any value created to date, and checks that any gaps left by the cancellation of

the project are raised to corporate or programme management.

prerequisites (plan)

Any fundamental aspects that must be in place, and remain in place, for a plan to succeed.

PRINCE2

A method that supports some selected aspects of project management. The acronym stands for Projects in a Controlled Environment.

PRINCE2 principles

The guiding obligations for good project management practice that form the basis of a project being managed using PRINCE2.

problem/concern

A type of issue (other than a request for change or off-specification) that the project manager needs to resolve or escalate.

procedure

A series of actions for a particular aspect of project management established specifically for the project – for example, a risk management procedure.

process

A structured set of activities designed to accomplish a specific objective. A process takes one or more defined inputs and turns them into defined outputs.

product

An input or output, whether tangible or intangible, that can be described in advance, created and tested. PRINCE2 has two types of products – management products and specialist products.

product description

A description of a product's purpose, composition, derivation and quality criteria. It is produced at planning time, as soon as possible after the need for the product is identified.

product status account

A report on the status of products. The required products can be specified by identifier or the part of the project in which they were developed.

product-based planning

A technique leading to a comprehensive plan based on the creation and delivery of required outputs. The technique considers prerequisite products, quality requirements and the dependencies between products.

programme

A temporary flexible organization structure created to coordinate, direct and oversee the implementation of a set of related projects and activities in order to deliver outcomes and benefits related to the organization's strategic objectives. A programme is likely to have a life that spans several years.

project

A temporary organization that is created for the purpose of delivering one or more business products according to an agreed business case.

project assurance

The project board's responsibilities to assure itself that the project is being conducted correctly. The project board members each have a specific area of focus for project assurance, namely business assurance for the executive, user assurance for the senior user(s), and supplier assurance for the senior supplier(s).

project initiation documentation

A logical set of documents that brings together the key information needed to start the project on a sound basis and that conveys the information to all concerned with the project.

project lifecycle

The period from the start-up of a project to the acceptance of the project product.

project management

The planning, delegating, monitoring and control of all aspects of the project, and the motivation of those involved, to achieve the project objectives within the expected performance targets for time, cost, quality, scope, benefits and risks.

project management team

The entire management structure of the project board, and project manager, plus any team manager, project assurance and project support roles.

project manager

The person given the authority and responsibility to manage the project on a day-to-day basis to deliver the required products within the constraints agreed with the project board.

project mandate

An external product generated by the authority commissioning the project that forms the trigger for Starting up a Project.

project office

A temporary office set up to support the delivery of a specific change initiative being delivered as a project. If used, the project office undertakes the responsibility of the project support role.

project plan

A high-level plan showing the major products of the project, when they will be delivered and at what cost. An initial project plan is presented as part of the project initiation documentation. This is revised as information on actual progress appears. It is a major control document for the project board to measure actual progress against expectations.

quality

The totality of features and inherent or assigned characteristics of a product, person, process, service and/or system that bears on its ability to show that it meets expectations or satisfies stated needs, requirements or specifications.

quality assurance

An independent check that products will be fit for purpose or meet requirements.

quality criteria

A description of the quality specification that the product must meet, and the quality measurements that will be applied by those inspecting the finished product.

quality management

The coordinated activities to direct and control an organization with regard to quality.

quality management strategy

A strategy defining the quality techniques and standards to be applied, and the various responsibilities for achieving the required quality levels, during a project.

quality management system

The complete set of quality standards, procedures and responsibilities for a site or organization. In the project context, 'sites' and 'organizations' should be interpreted as the permanent or semi-permanent organization(s) sponsoring the project work, i.e. they are 'external' to the project's temporary organization. A programme, for instance, can be regarded as a semi-permanent organization that sponsors projects – and it may have a documented quality management system.

quality register

A register containing summary details of all planned and completed quality activities. The quality register is used by the project manager and project assurance as part of reviewing progress.

quality review technique

A quality inspection technique with defined roles and a specific structure. It is designed to assess whether a product that takes the form of a document (or similar, e.g. a presentation) is complete, adheres to standards and meets the quality criteria agreed for it in the relevant product description. The participants are drawn from those with the necessary competence to evaluate its fitness for purpose.

release

The set of products in a handover. The contents of a release are managed, tested and deployed as a single entity. See also 'handover'.

request for change

A proposal for a change to a baseline. It is a type of issue.

risk

An uncertain event or set of events that, should it occur, will have an effect on the achievement of objectives. A risk is measured by a combination of the probability of a perceived threat or opportunity occurring, and the magnitude of its impact on objectives.

risk management

The systematic application of principles, approaches and processes to the tasks of identifying and assessing risks, and then planning and implementing risk responses.

risk register

A record of identified risks relating to an initiative, including their status and history.

role description

A description of the set of responsibilities specific to a role.

schedule

Graphical representation of a plan (for example, a Gantt chart), typically describing a sequence of tasks, together with resource allocations, which collectively deliver the plan. In PRINCE2, project activities should only be documented in the schedules associated with a project plan, stage plan or team plan. Actions that are allocated from day-to-day management may be documented in the relevant project log (i.e. risk register, daily log, issue register, quality register) if they do not require significant activity.

scope

For a plan, the sum total of its products and the extent of their requirements. It is described by the product breakdown structure for the plan and associated product descriptions.

senior responsible owner

A UK government term for the individual responsible for ensuring that a project or programme of change meets its objectives and delivers the projected benefits. The person should be the owner of the overall business change that is being supported by the project. The senior responsible owner (SRO) should ensure that the change maintains its business focus, that it has clear authority, and that the context, including risks, is actively managed. This individual must be senior and must take personal responsibility for successful delivery of the project. The SRO should be recognized as the owner throughout the organization.

The SRO appoints the project's executive (or in some cases may elect to be the executive).

senior supplier

The project board role that provides knowledge and experience of the main discipline(s) involved in the production of the project's deliverable(s). The senior supplier represents the supplier interests within the project and provides supplier resources.

senior user

The project board role accountable for ensuring that user needs are specified correctly and that the solution meets those needs.

sponsor

The main driving force behind a programme or project. PRINCE2 does not define a role for the sponsor, but the sponsor is most likely to be the executive on the project board, or the person who has appointed the executive.

stage plan

A detailed plan used as the basis for project management control throughout a stage.

stakeholder

Any individual, group or organization that can affect, be affected by, or perceive itself to be affected by, an initiative (programme, project, activity, risk).

supplier

The person, group or groups responsible for the supply of the project's specialist products.

tailoring

The appropriate use of PRINCE2 on any given project, ensuring that there is the correct amount of planning, control, governance and use of the processes and themes (whereas the adoption of PRINCE2 across an organization is known as 'embedding').

team manager

The person responsible for the production of those products allocated by the project manager (as defined in a work package) to an appropriate quality, timescale and at a cost acceptable to the project board. This role reports to, and takes direction from, the project manager. If a team manager is not assigned, then the project manager undertakes the responsibilities of the team manager role.

team plan

An optional level of plan used as the basis for team management control when executing work packages.

theme

An aspect of project management that needs to be continually addressed, and that requires specific treatment for the PRINCE2 processes to be effective.

tolerance

The permissible deviation above and below a plan's target for time and cost without escalating the deviation to the next level of management. There may also be tolerance levels for quality, scope, benefit and risk. Tolerance is applied at project, stage and team levels.

user acceptance

A specific type of acceptance by the person or group who will use the product once it is handed over into the operational environment.

user

The person or group who will use one or more of the project's products.

version

A specific baseline of a product. Versions typically use naming conventions that enable the sequence or date of the baseline to be identified. For example, project plan version 2 is the baseline after project plan version 1.

waterfall method

A development approach that is linear and sequential with distinct goals for each phase of development. Once a phase of development is completed, the development proceeds to the next phase and earlier phases are not revisited (hence the analogy that water flowing down a mountain cannot go back).

work package

The set of information relevant to the creation of one or more products. It will contain a description of the work, the product description(s), details of any constraints on production, and confirmation of the agreement between the project manager and the person or team manager who is to implement the work package that the work can be done within the constraints.

Index

Index